Alex Billington

Alex Billington

HOW IT WORKS

THE
ENVIRONMENT

Michael Allaby

HORUS EDITIONS

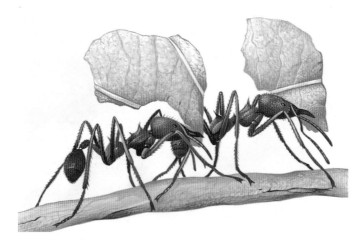

Illustrated by Mike Saunders; Jim Channell; Gary Hincks;
Ruth Lindsay; Brian Pearce and David Wright

ISBN 1-899762-37-X

Copyright © 1996 Horus Editions Limited

First published 1996
This edition first published 1997
Sixth impression 2004

Published by Horus Editions Limited,
1st Floor, 27 Longford Street,
London, NW1 3DZ

Printed in Singapore

HOW IT WORKS

CONTENTS

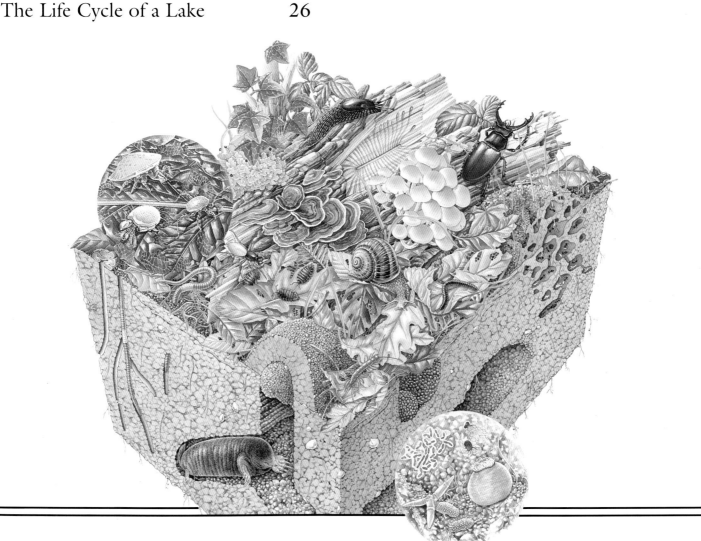

What is the Environment?

WE CAN think of the whole of planet Earth as the environment. An environment is a place in which living things can find food and shelter. It consists of the surroundings (the rocks, soil, air and water) and the living things themselves. On Earth, life is possible almost everywhere – on dry land, and from the deepest ocean floor to the lower part of the atmosphere. But rather than look at this complete environment it is often easier to look at smaller, more local parts of it.

Two other planets, Mars and Venus, are like our Earth in many ways, but nothing can live on them. One day humans may live on Mars, but to do so they will have to alter the surroundings to make them Earth-like. They will have to create an environment.

NEARLY 9 KILOMETRES HIGH, MOUNT EVEREST JUST REACHES THE STRATOSPHERE

THE CRUST IS MADE OF LARGE PLATES THAT MOVE, CAUSING CRACKS, RIDGES AND MOUNTAINS

THE ENVIRONMENT STRETCHES FROM THE BOTTOM OF THE OCEANS TO THE TOP OF THE TROPOSPHERE

THE OUTER MANTLE CONTAINS MOLTEN ROCK THAT SOMETIMES ERUPTS FROM VOLCANOES

THE OUTER CORE IS VERY HOT – THE TEMPERATURE IS OVER 5,000°C

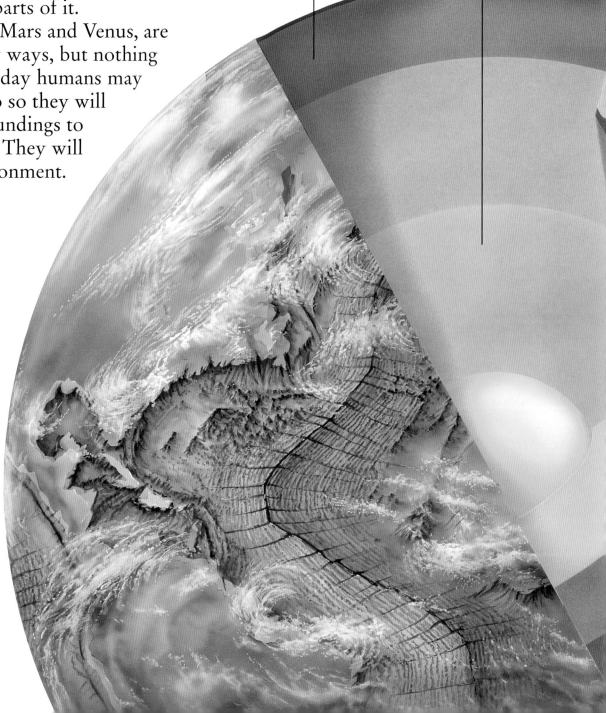

Planet Earth
The environment that surrounds us is tiny compared to the depth of the Earth beneath. The Earth is formed in layers. The inner layers are very hot and around 1,000–2,000 kilometres thick. At the centre of the Earth the inner core is made of hot solid metal. This is covered by the outer core, a layer of molten metal. Around the outer core are the inner and outer mantles made of semi-molten rock. The soil and rock on which we live are called the crust – a layer only 5 to 60 kilometres thick. Above, the atmosphere forms a thin outer covering around the Earth.

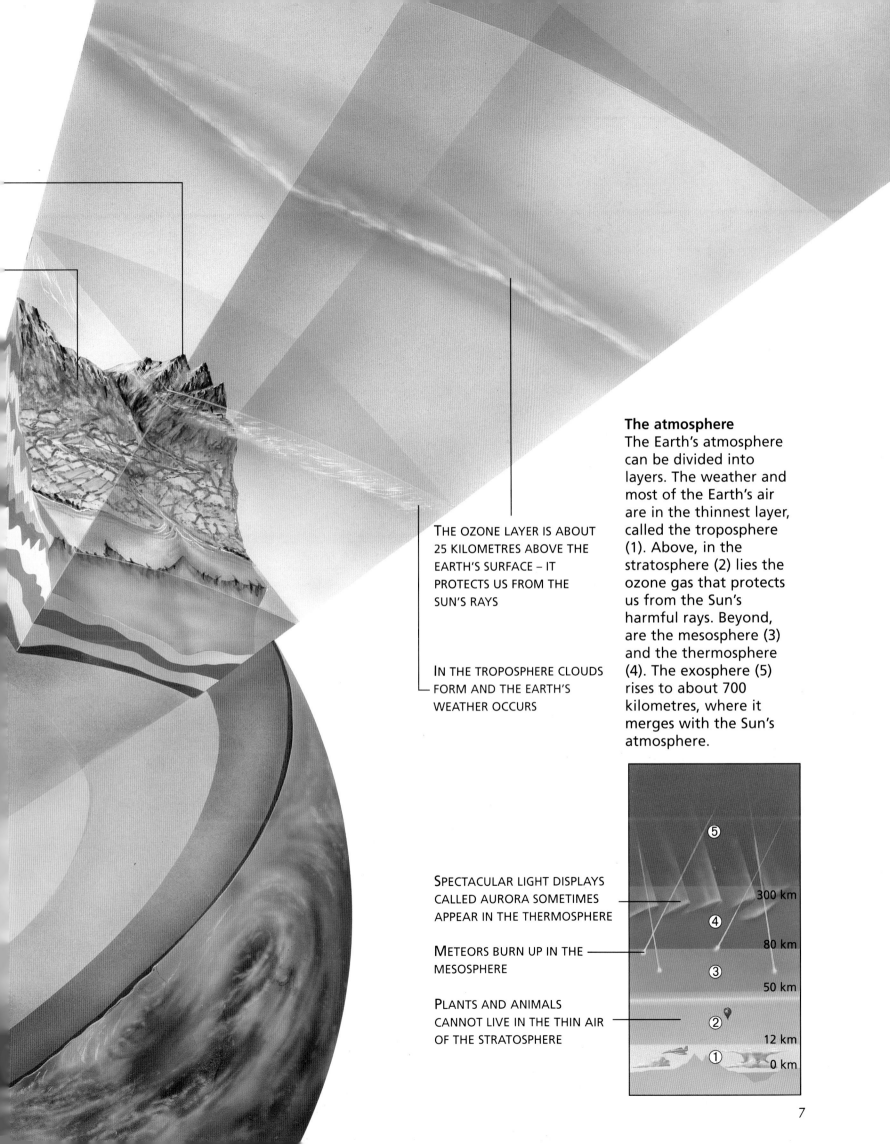

THE OZONE LAYER IS ABOUT
25 KILOMETRES ABOVE THE
EARTH'S SURFACE – IT
PROTECTS US FROM THE
SUN'S RAYS

IN THE TROPOSPHERE CLOUDS
FORM AND THE EARTH'S
WEATHER OCCURS

The atmosphere
The Earth's atmosphere
can be divided into
layers. The weather and
most of the Earth's air
are in the thinnest layer,
called the troposphere
(1). Above, in the
stratosphere (2) lies the
ozone gas that protects
us from the Sun's
harmful rays. Beyond,
are the mesosphere (3)
and the thermosphere
(4). The exosphere (5)
rises to about 700
kilometres, where it
merges with the Sun's
atmosphere.

SPECTACULAR LIGHT DISPLAYS
CALLED AURORA SOMETIMES
APPEAR IN THE THERMOSPHERE

METEORS BURN UP IN THE
MESOSPHERE

PLANTS AND ANIMALS
CANNOT LIVE IN THE THIN AIR
OF THE STRATOSPHERE

⑤

300 km

④

80 km

③

50 km

②

12 km

①

0 km

Air and Water

AIR AND water change the environment. Along with sunshine they affect climate, the weather and the type of vegetation that grows. At the equator the Sun is almost directly overhead at noon, so places on and near the equator are warmed more strongly than elsewhere. When heated the air moves away from the equator. At the same time cooler air moves towards the equator. This circulation of the air brings us weather. The Earth's winds are a part of this air circulation. Ocean waters, in warm or cold currents, also affect climates because air is warmed or cooled as it passes over them.

Climate

Climate is the range of weather conditions found in a particular area. Generally, the further you go from the equator, the colder the climate becomes. The climate of a region affects the type of vegetation found there. Rain forests (1) grow near the equator where the climate is hot and wet. Deserts (2) are in hot, dry climates. Temperate forests (3) grow in mild climates, while evergreen forests (4) are often found in colder climates. In polar regions (5) there is little vegetation because the climate is dry and very cold.

SOUTH POLE

8

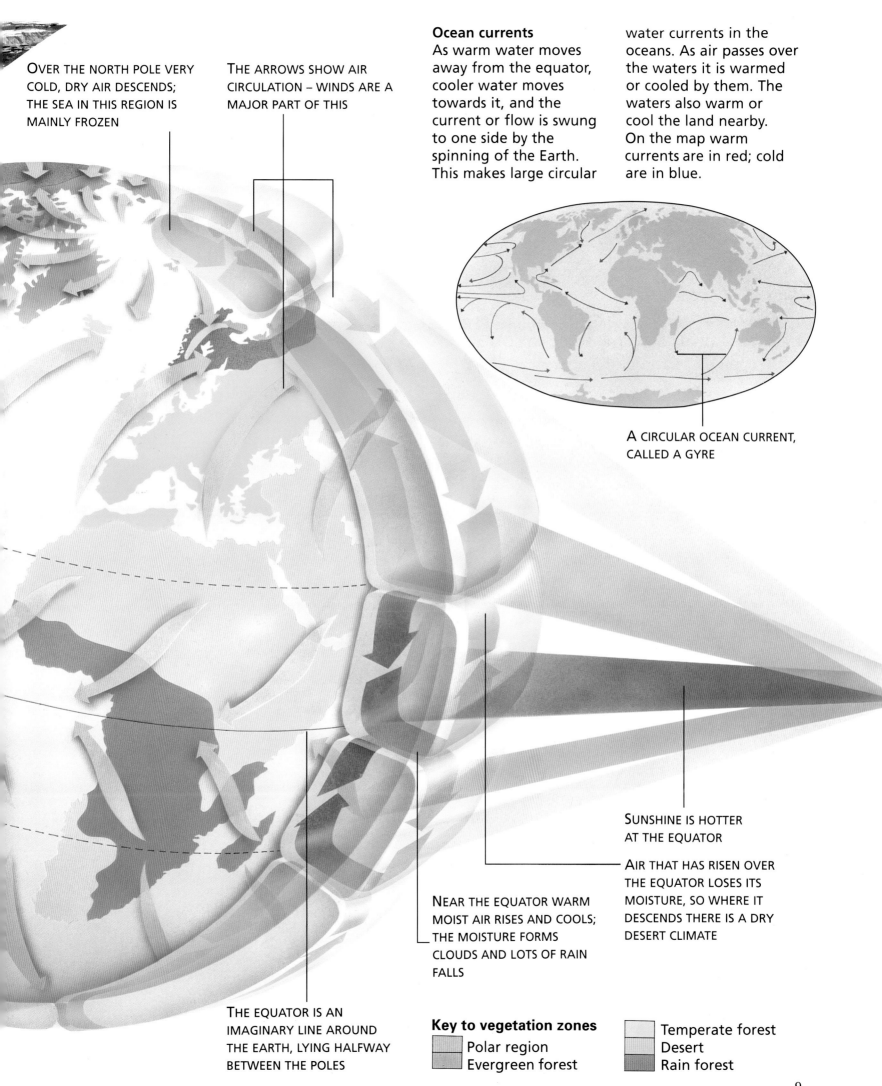

OVER THE NORTH POLE VERY COLD, DRY AIR DESCENDS; THE SEA IN THIS REGION IS MAINLY FROZEN

THE ARROWS SHOW AIR CIRCULATION – WINDS ARE A MAJOR PART OF THIS

Ocean currents
As warm water moves away from the equator, cooler water moves towards it, and the current or flow is swung to one side by the spinning of the Earth. This makes large circular water currents in the oceans. As air passes over the waters it is warmed or cooled by them. The waters also warm or cool the land nearby. On the map warm currents are in red; cold are in blue.

A CIRCULAR OCEAN CURRENT, CALLED A GYRE

SUNSHINE IS HOTTER AT THE EQUATOR

AIR THAT HAS RISEN OVER THE EQUATOR LOSES ITS MOISTURE, SO WHERE IT DESCENDS THERE IS A DRY DESERT CLIMATE

NEAR THE EQUATOR WARM MOIST AIR RISES AND COOLS; THE MOISTURE FORMS CLOUDS AND LOTS OF RAIN FALLS

THE EQUATOR IS AN IMAGINARY LINE AROUND THE EARTH, LYING HALFWAY BETWEEN THE POLES

Key to vegetation zones
Polar region
Evergreen forest
Temperate forest
Desert
Rain forest

The Ozone Layer

SUNLIGHT, which we see as white, is really a mixture of the colours in a rainbow. The Sun also radiates light which we cannot see, some of it called ultraviolet (UV) light.

If too much UV light reaches the Earth's surface it is harmful and can cause skin cancer. However, a layer of ozone gas in the atmosphere protects us by absorbing some of the UV light. But in some parts of the world, particularly over Antarctica, the ozone layer has become thinner, allowing more UV light to reach the Earth.

THE OZONE LAYER, WHERE OZONE GATHERS, IS 20–25 KILOMETRES ABOVE THE GROUND

AS IT PASSES THROUGH THE OZONE LAYER SOME UV LIGHT IS ABSORBED BY OZONE

A THINNING OF THE OZONE LAYER IS SOMETIMES DESCRIBED AS AN 'OZONE HOLE'

WHERE THE OZONE LAYER IS THIN, MORE UV LIGHT REACHES THE GROUND

TOO MUCH UV LIGHT CAUSES SUNBURN AND SKIN CANCER

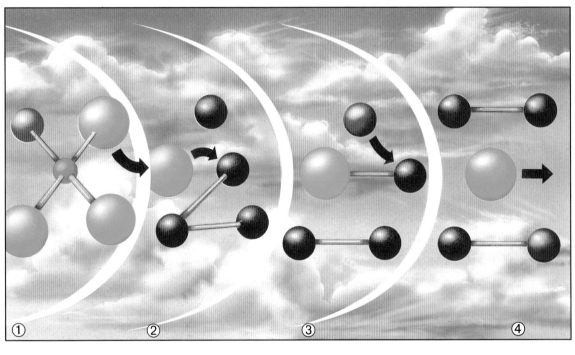

① ② ③ ④

Ozone breakdown

In the ozone layer there are gases which have chlorine atoms in their molecules. These gases include CFCs (chloro-fluorocarbons). A CFC molecule with its chlorine atoms is pictured above (1). The chlorine atoms are coloured green.

UV light from the Sun breaks these CFC molecules up, and the chlorine atoms break off and float away. In winter over Antarctica, fierce winds blow around a centre of still air. As winter draws to an end, clouds of ice crystals form in the still air. On the surface of these crystals, the free chlorine atoms join up with ozone molecules (2). This removes an oxygen atom (red) from the ozone molecule, and breaks the molecule up. The spare oxygen atom then leaves the chlorine to join another spare oxygen atom (3). The chlorine is then free to break down another ozone molecule (4). This reduces the amount of ozone in the ozone layer, making an ozone 'hole'. Until recently CFCs have been widely used – in aerosol cans and refrigerators, for example. Now people know that CFCs destroy ozone, their use is being stopped.

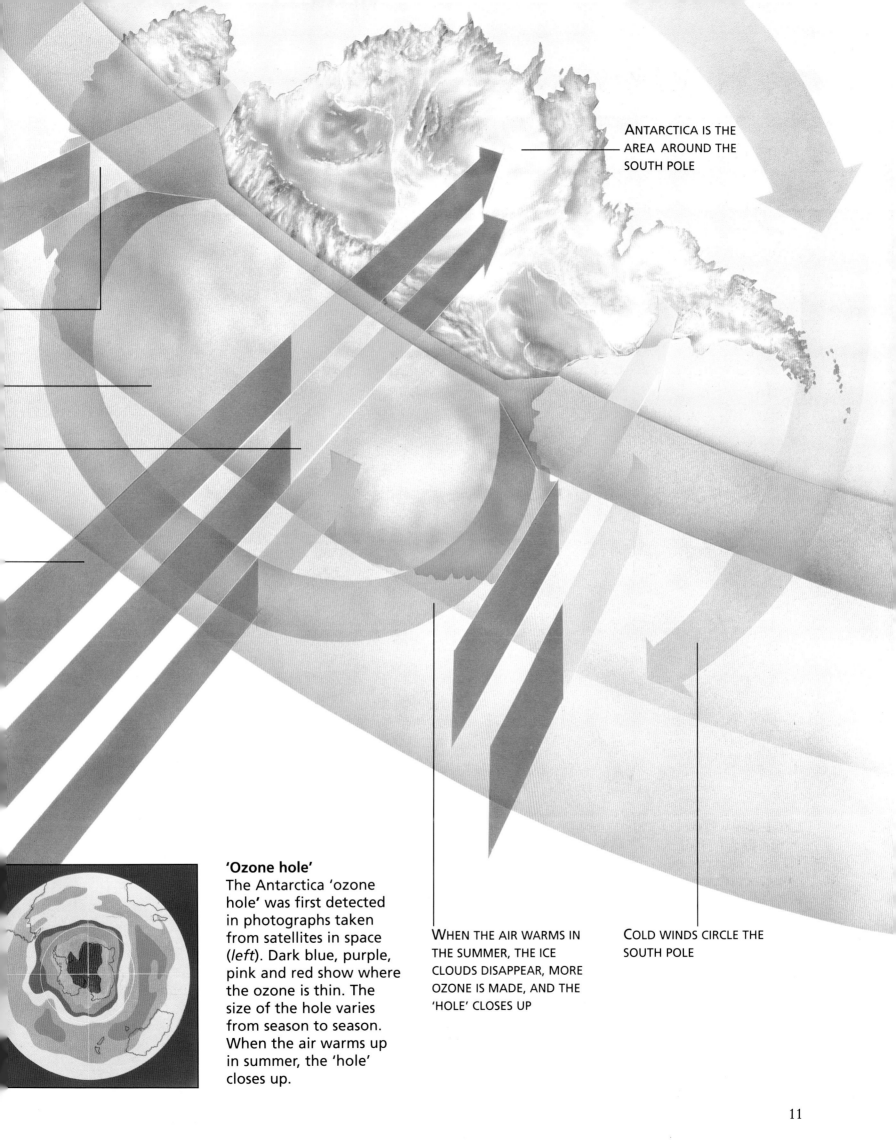

ANTARCTICA IS THE AREA AROUND THE SOUTH POLE

'Ozone hole'
The Antarctica 'ozone hole' was first detected in photographs taken from satellites in space (*left*). Dark blue, purple, pink and red show where the ozone is thin. The size of the hole varies from season to season. When the air warms up in summer, the 'hole' closes up.

WHEN THE AIR WARMS IN THE SUMMER, THE ICE CLOUDS DISAPPEAR, MORE OZONE IS MADE, AND THE 'HOLE' CLOSES UP

COLD WINDS CIRCLE THE SOUTH POLE

The Greenhouse Effect

THE SUN'S rays pass through the air freely, without warming it. When they reach the surfaces of the ground and sea, the surfaces are warmed. These surfaces then send heat back up into the sky, warming the air. Unlike the incoming Sun's rays, the outgoing heat warms some of the gases in the air. These 'greenhouse' gases are like a blanket holding in heat that would otherwise escape into outer space. This is called the 'greenhouse effect' because, like the glass of a greenhouse, the gases allow energy to pass more easily inwards than outwards. Many industries produce greenhouse gases.

POWER STATIONS BURNING COAL OR NATURAL GAS EMIT GREENHOUSE GASES

THE MOST IMPORTANT GREENHOUSE GAS IS CARBON DIOXIDE

SOME SCIENTISTS BELIEVE THE RELEASE OF GREENHOUSE GASES SHOULD BE REDUCED, OR THE EARTH'S CLIMATE WILL GET HOTTER

CARS, BURNING PETROL, RELEASE CARBON DIOXIDE AS WELL AS NITROUS OXIDE, ANOTHER GREENHOUSE GAS

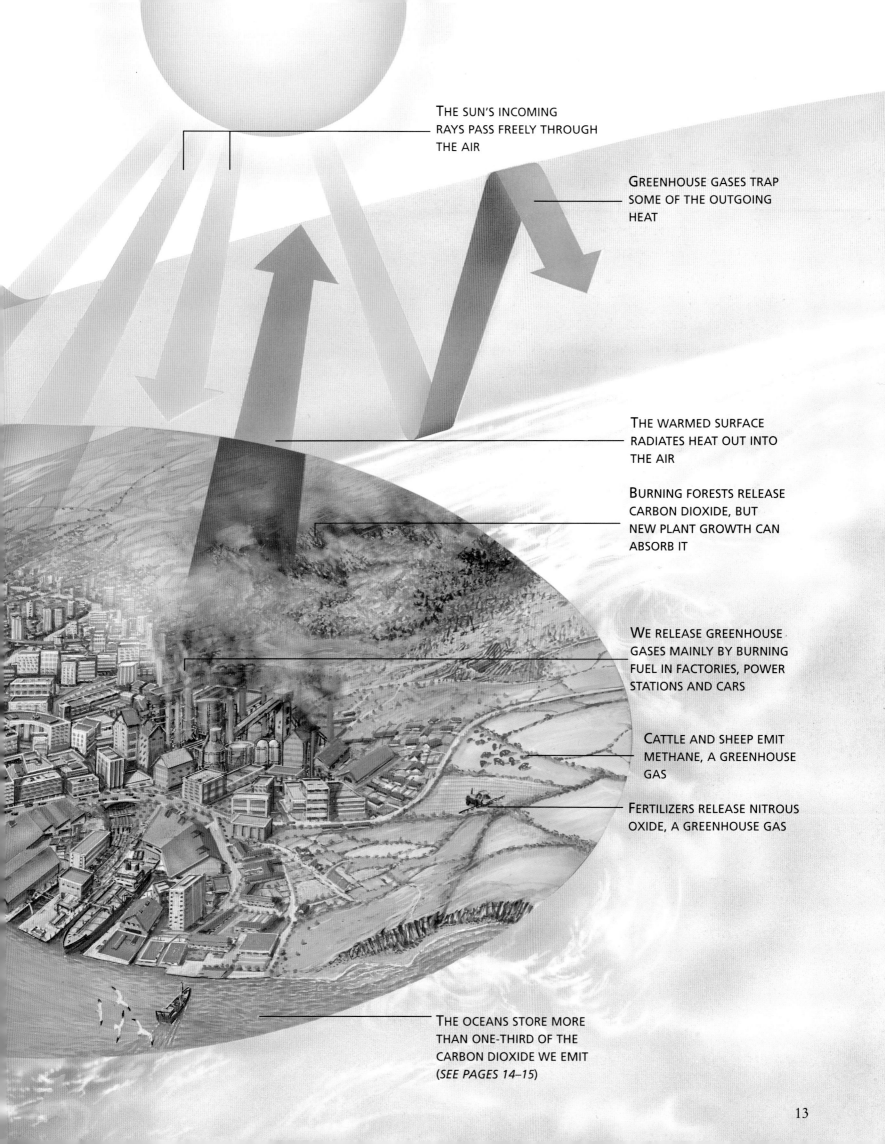

THE SUN'S INCOMING RAYS PASS FREELY THROUGH THE AIR

GREENHOUSE GASES TRAP SOME OF THE OUTGOING HEAT

THE WARMED SURFACE RADIATES HEAT OUT INTO THE AIR

BURNING FORESTS RELEASE CARBON DIOXIDE, BUT NEW PLANT GROWTH CAN ABSORB IT

WE RELEASE GREENHOUSE GASES MAINLY BY BURNING FUEL IN FACTORIES, POWER STATIONS AND CARS

CATTLE AND SHEEP EMIT METHANE, A GREENHOUSE GAS

FERTILIZERS RELEASE NITROUS OXIDE, A GREENHOUSE GAS

THE OCEANS STORE MORE THAN ONE-THIRD OF THE CARBON DIOXIDE WE EMIT (*SEE PAGES 14–15*)

Gaia, The Living Earth

ALL LIVING organisms alter the chemistry of their environment. When we breathe we remove a little oxygen from the air and add a little carbon dioxide. After digesting food our body rids itself of waste. These two events alone alter the environment.

In 1979 a British scientist, James Lovelock, proposed the Gaia theory. On a 'living' planet, organisms alter their environment, managing or regulating it. In this way, said Lovelock, the Earth regulates itself, making sure there is enough oxygen for animals and carbon dioxide for plants, for example. Shown here is the way in which tiny marine plants and shellfish regulate the Earth's temperature and the amount of carbon dioxide (CO_2) in the air.

Carbon dioxide
Carbon dioxide is a greenhouse gas (*see pages 12–13*). It dissolves in rain and then enters the sea. There, tiny plants and animals use it to make their shells of calcium carbonate. When the organisms die, their shells fall to the seabed. Eventually these are ground down, and form chalk and limestone rocks. Such rocks are very common and often contain fossils of the shells.

This whole process removes carbon dioxide from the air and helps stop the Earth from growing warmer. The average temperature on Earth has always been about 15°C.

CHALK CLIFFS WERE FORMED OVER MILLIONS OF YEARS BY DEAD MARINE ORGANISMS

CHALK CLIFFS ARE LIKE GIANT STOREHOUSES FOR CO_2 – STORED AS CALCIUM CARBONATE

AS DEAD SHELLFISH AND TINY ORGANISMS DIE AND BREAK UP, SOME CARBON DIOXIDE (CO_2) IS RELEASED

WHEN SEA ORGANISMS DIE THEIR BONES AND SHELLS MAKE A CHALKY SEDIMENT

THE SEDIMENT BECOMES CHALK OR LIMESTONE ROCK, WHICH WILL EVENTUALLY BE THRUST ABOVE THE SURFACE OF THE SEA

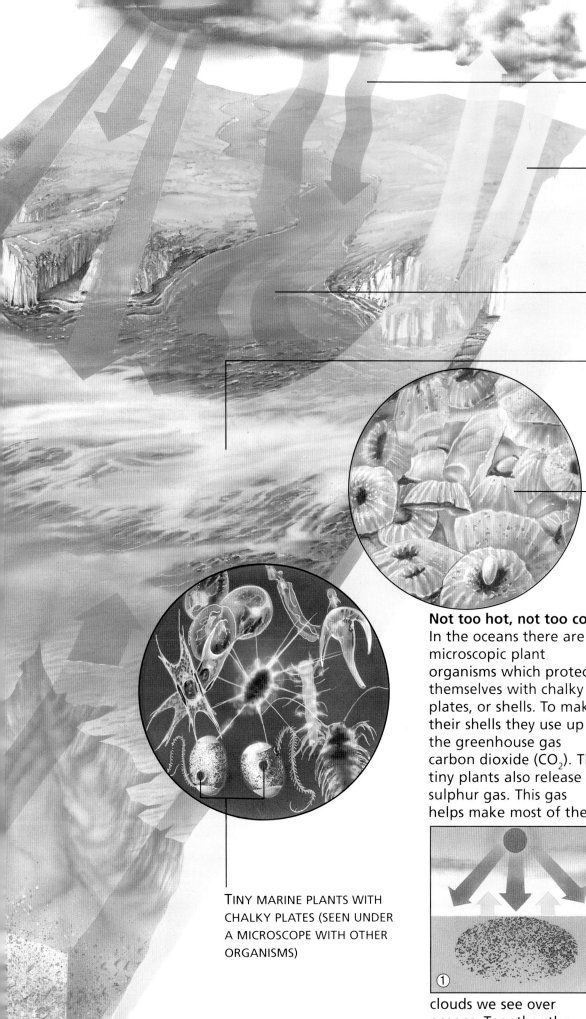

CO₂ MOVES FROM THE AIR AND THROUGH RIVERS TO THE SEA

MORE SULPHUR IS RELEASED AS MARINE ORGANISMS GROW – THIS PRODUCES MORE CLOUDS, AND MAKES TEMPERATURES FALL

SEA ORGANISMS USE CO₂ TO MAKE THEIR BONES AND SHELLS

MICROSCOPIC PLANTS (CALLED PHYTOPLANKTON) GIVE THE SEA A CREAMY APPEARANCE BECAUSE OF THEIR CHALKY SHELLS

UNDER A MICROSCOPE THE FOSSILS OF TINY MARINE PLANTS AND SHELLS CAN BE SEEN IN CHALK

TINY MARINE PLANTS WITH CHALKY PLATES (SEEN UNDER A MICROSCOPE WITH OTHER ORGANISMS)

Not too hot, not too cold

In the oceans there are microscopic plant organisms which protect themselves with chalky plates, or shells. To make their shells they use up the greenhouse gas carbon dioxide (CO_2). The tiny plants also release a sulphur gas. This gas helps make most of the

clouds we see over oceans. Together these processes help regulate the Earth's temperature.

When skies are clear the Sun's rays warm the Earth and its waters. The ocean's tiny plants then multiply faster and remove more CO_2 from the air. The multiplying plants also release more sulphur, which makes clouds form, cooling the ocean surface (1). As the water temperature cools, the tiny plants begin to die, and as they

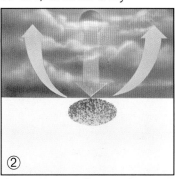

decompose they release CO_2 back into the air (2). The amount of sulphur is reduced, the skies clear, the ocean warms up, and the cycle begins again.

Plant Life

PLANTS are among the few living things on Earth that can make their own food. They do this by a process called photosynthesis. Sunlight falling on the plant's leaves is captured by chlorophyll, the substance in the cells that gives the plant its green colour. Energy from the light is used to combine water and carbon dioxide to make food in the form of sugars. This food is then transported to all the other parts of the plant, providing the energy it needs to live and grow. Plants also use energy in taking the minerals they need from the soil to build their cells. The byproduct of photosynthesis is oxygen, which passes out of the plant through its leaves.

SUNLIGHT FALLS ON PLANT LEAVES

CHLOROPHYLL CAPTURES THE SUNLIGHT

IN PHOTOSYNTHESIS OXYGEN IS RELEASED INTO THE ATMOSPHERE

LEAVES ARE GREEN BECAUSE THEY CONTAIN CHLOROPHYLL

WATER TRAVELS UP VESSELS IN THE STEM

WATER AND NUTRIENTS TAKEN UP FROM THE SOIL ENTER THROUGH THE ROOTS

CARBON DIOXIDE FROM THE ATMOSPHERE ENTERS THROUGH STOMATA IN THE LEAF

CARBON DIOXIDE, OXYGEN AND WATER VAPOUR PASS THROUGH STOMATA

WATER TRAVELS THROUGH THESE TUBES

PHOTOSYNTHESIS TAKES PLACE IN CHLOROPHYLL INSIDE THE CYLINDRICAL CELLS

SUGARS ARE STORED IN THE MESOPHYLL LAYER

THE PALISADE

Respiration

All plants, like animals, continuously respire. Respiration is almost the reverse of photosynthesis: oxygen is taken in and carbon dioxide is released. The oxygen is used to break down the sugars the plant has made to produce the energy it needs to live.

During the day photosynthesis occurs faster than respiration so more carbon dioxide is taken in than released. At night photosynthesis stops and carbon dioxide is not taken in; it is only released, through respiration.

AT NIGHT ONLY CARBON DIOXIDE AND WATER VAPOUR ARE RELEASED

Inside the leaf

This high-magnification cross-section of a leaf shows the cells, where photosynthesis takes place. Water vapour, oxygen and carbon dioxide enter and leave through tiny holes (called stomata) found mainly on the lower surface. Sunlight is taken in by the cylindrical cells in the palisade layer. The sugars made are then stored in the spongy mesophyll layer beneath, before being transported to other parts of the plant.

17

Food Webs

G REEN plants make their own food (*see pages 16–17*). They are the first in a line of organisms, along which food-energy is passed. This line is called a 'food chain'. Plants, the 'primary producers', are the first link in the chain. The second link is plant-eating animals, called 'primary consumers'. Animals that eat other animals (meat-eaters) are next. They are called 'secondary consumers'.

In a community of plants and animals there are lots of food chains and many are connected. When each food is linked to the animal eating it, a 'food web' appears like the one shown here.

Food chains

Most food chains begin with green plants. Plant-eaters, such as rabbits, eat the plants. Digesting their food, moving and keeping warm or cool uses up nine-tenths of the energy in the food. So a meat-eater, such as a fox, gets only one-tenth of the food energy eaten by a rabbit. This energy loss can be shown as a pyramid.

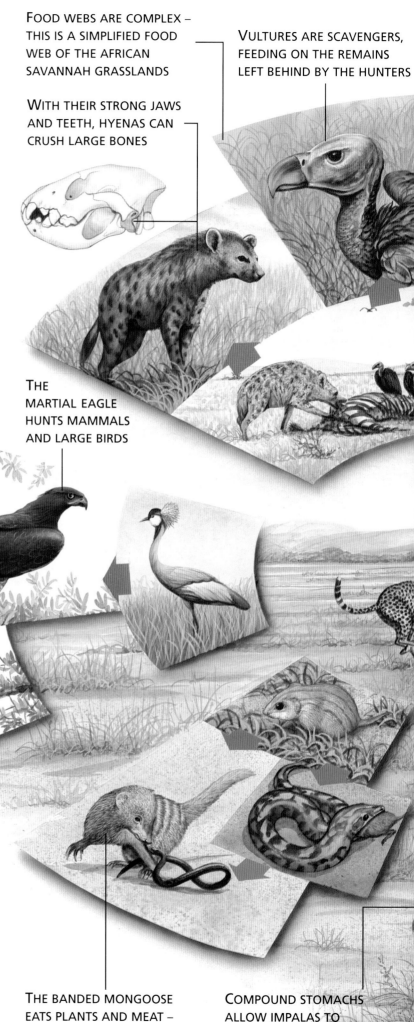

FOOD WEBS ARE COMPLEX – THIS IS A SIMPLIFIED FOOD WEB OF THE AFRICAN SAVANNAH GRASSLANDS

VULTURES ARE SCAVENGERS, FEEDING ON THE REMAINS LEFT BEHIND BY THE HUNTERS

WITH THEIR STRONG JAWS AND TEETH, HYENAS CAN CRUSH LARGE BONES

THE MARTIAL EAGLE HUNTS MAMMALS AND LARGE BIRDS

A BEE-EATER

THE BANDED MONGOOSE EATS PLANTS AND MEAT – IT IS AN OMNIVORE

COMPOUND STOMACHS ALLOW IMPALAS TO DIGEST GRASS

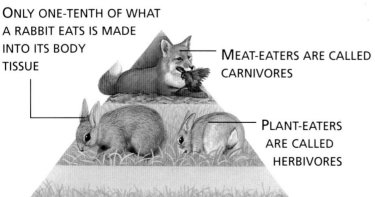

ONLY ONE-TENTH OF WHAT A RABBIT EATS IS MADE INTO ITS BODY TISSUE

MEAT-EATERS ARE CALLED CARNIVORES

PLANT-EATERS ARE CALLED HERBIVORES

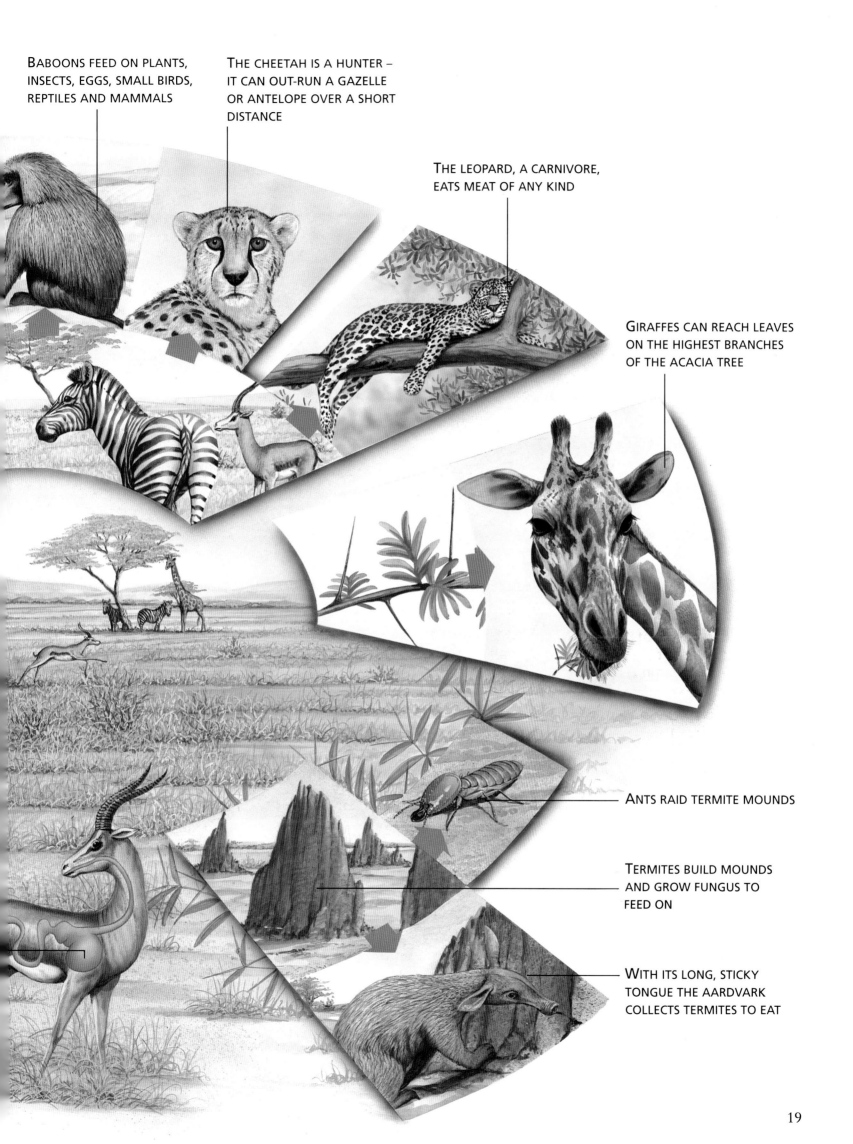

BABOONS FEED ON PLANTS, INSECTS, EGGS, SMALL BIRDS, REPTILES AND MAMMALS

THE CHEETAH IS A HUNTER – IT CAN OUT-RUN A GAZELLE OR ANTELOPE OVER A SHORT DISTANCE

THE LEOPARD, A CARNIVORE, EATS MEAT OF ANY KIND

GIRAFFES CAN REACH LEAVES ON THE HIGHEST BRANCHES OF THE ACACIA TREE

ANTS RAID TERMITE MOUNDS

TERMITES BUILD MOUNDS AND GROW FUNGUS TO FEED ON

WITH ITS LONG, STICKY TONGUE THE AARDVARK COLLECTS TERMITES TO EAT

19

The Living Oceans

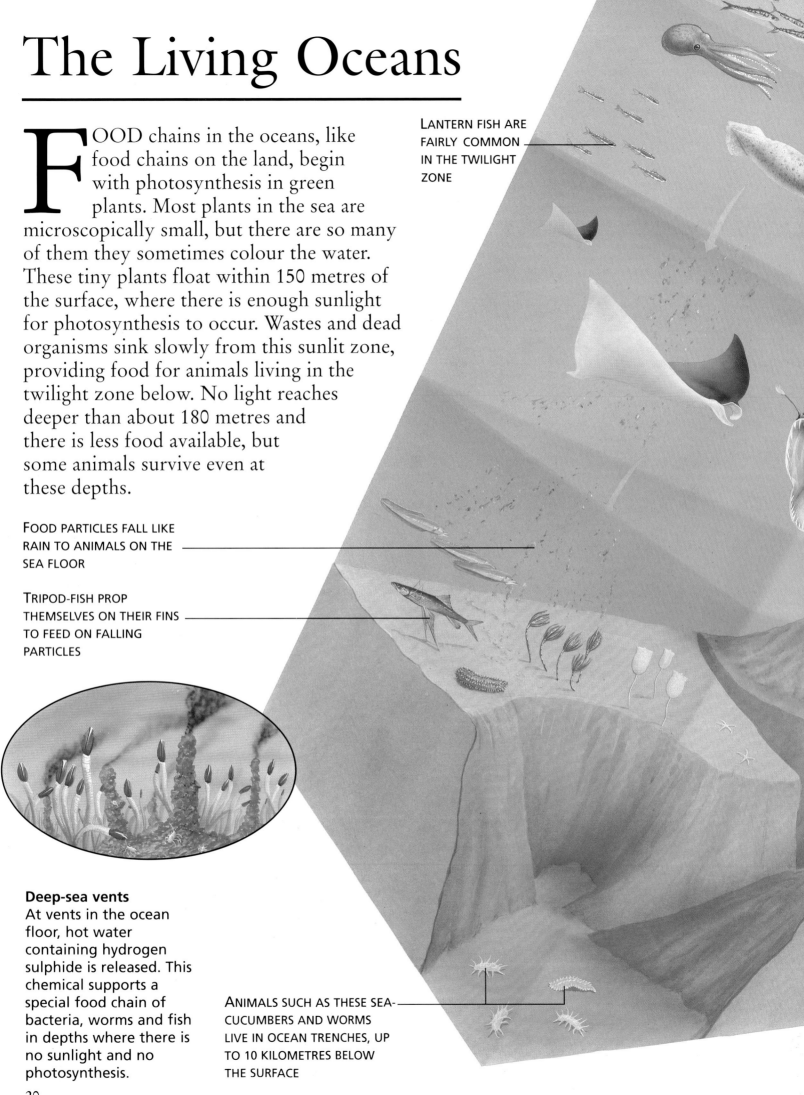

FOOD chains in the oceans, like food chains on the land, begin with photosynthesis in green plants. Most plants in the sea are microscopically small, but there are so many of them they sometimes colour the water. These tiny plants float within 150 metres of the surface, where there is enough sunlight for photosynthesis to occur. Wastes and dead organisms sink slowly from this sunlit zone, providing food for animals living in the twilight zone below. No light reaches deeper than about 180 metres and there is less food available, but some animals survive even at these depths.

LANTERN FISH ARE FAIRLY COMMON IN THE TWILIGHT ZONE

FOOD PARTICLES FALL LIKE RAIN TO ANIMALS ON THE SEA FLOOR

TRIPOD-FISH PROP THEMSELVES ON THEIR FINS TO FEED ON FALLING PARTICLES

Deep-sea vents
At vents in the ocean floor, hot water containing hydrogen sulphide is released. This chemical supports a special food chain of bacteria, worms and fish in depths where there is no sunlight and no photosynthesis.

ANIMALS SUCH AS THESE SEA-CUCUMBERS AND WORMS LIVE IN OCEAN TRENCHES, UP TO 10 KILOMETRES BELOW THE SURFACE

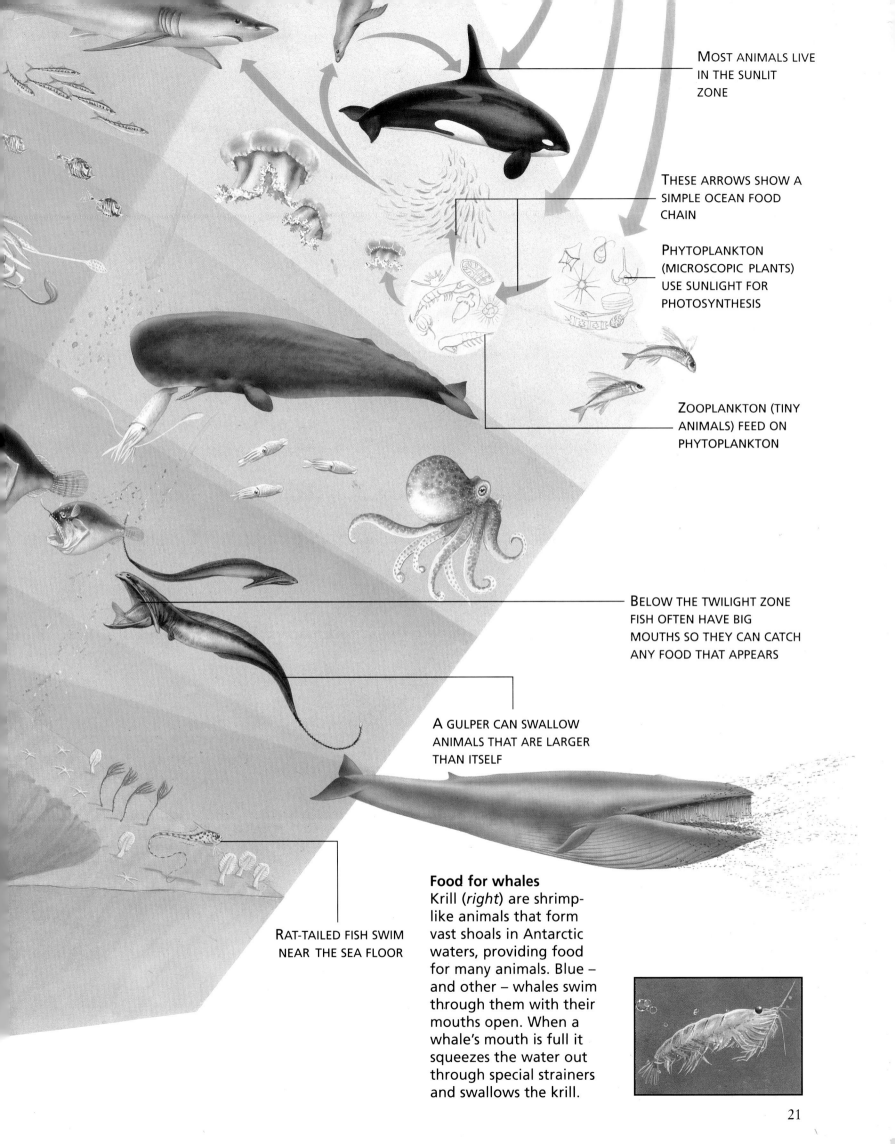

MOST ANIMALS LIVE IN THE SUNLIT ZONE

THESE ARROWS SHOW A SIMPLE OCEAN FOOD CHAIN

PHYTOPLANKTON (MICROSCOPIC PLANTS) USE SUNLIGHT FOR PHOTOSYNTHESIS

ZOOPLANKTON (TINY ANIMALS) FEED ON PHYTOPLANKTON

BELOW THE TWILIGHT ZONE FISH OFTEN HAVE BIG MOUTHS SO THEY CAN CATCH ANY FOOD THAT APPEARS

A GULPER CAN SWALLOW ANIMALS THAT ARE LARGER THAN ITSELF

RAT-TAILED FISH SWIM NEAR THE SEA FLOOR

Food for whales
Krill (*right*) are shrimp-like animals that form vast shoals in Antarctic waters, providing food for many animals. Blue – and other – whales swim through them with their mouths open. When a whale's mouth is full it squeezes the water out through special strainers and swallows the krill.

21

Migration

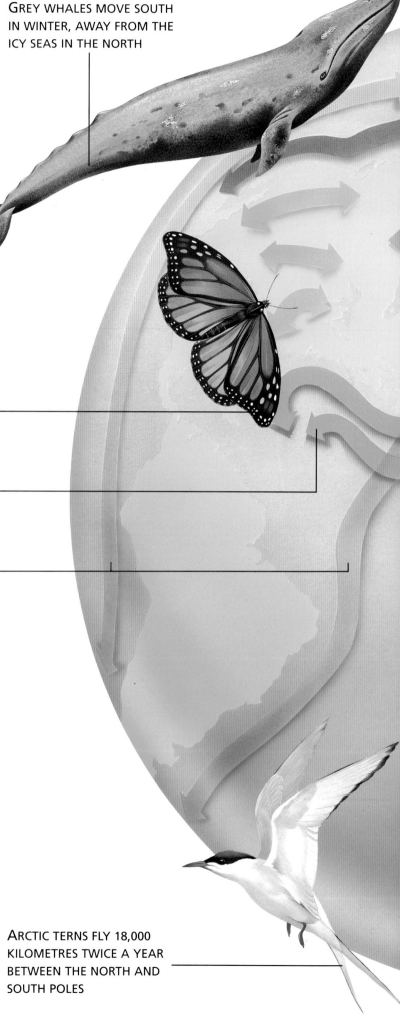

GREY WHALES MOVE SOUTH IN WINTER, AWAY FROM THE ICY SEAS IN THE NORTH

AT ALL PLACES other than the equator, the climates of the Earth are seasonal. This means that part of the year is too dry or too cold for plants to grow. But animals must eat, whether plants are growing or not. They must also make sure that their young are born in the right place and at the right time so they will be able to find enough food to feed them. Many animals avoid difficult seasons by migrating. Each year, when their food supply begins to run out, they make journeys, some of them very long.

EACH SPRING AND AUTUMN MONARCH BUTTERFLIES FLY NEARLY 3,000 KILOMETRES

Key to migration routes

- Monarch butterfly
- Grey whale
- Caribou
- Eel
- Swallow
- Wildebeest
- Arctic tern

EELS MIGRATE TO THE SARGASSO SEA

THE LONGEST MIGRATION IS THAT OF THE ARCTIC TERN – TWICE A YEAR IT FLIES FOR FOUR MONTHS NON-STOP

Seasons

The Earth takes a year to orbit the Sun and a day to turn on its own axis. This axis is not at right angles to the Sun's rays, so as the Earth orbits, first one hemisphere and then the other is tilted towards the Sun. This produces the seasons. The hemisphere facing the Sun experiences summer, while the other hemisphere has its winter.

HERE IT IS SUMMER IN THE NORTHERN HEMISPHERE

HERE IT IS SUMMER IN THE SOUTHERN HEMISPHERE

THE EARTH'S AXIS

ARCTIC TERNS FLY 18,000 KILOMETRES TWICE A YEAR BETWEEN THE NORTH AND SOUTH POLES

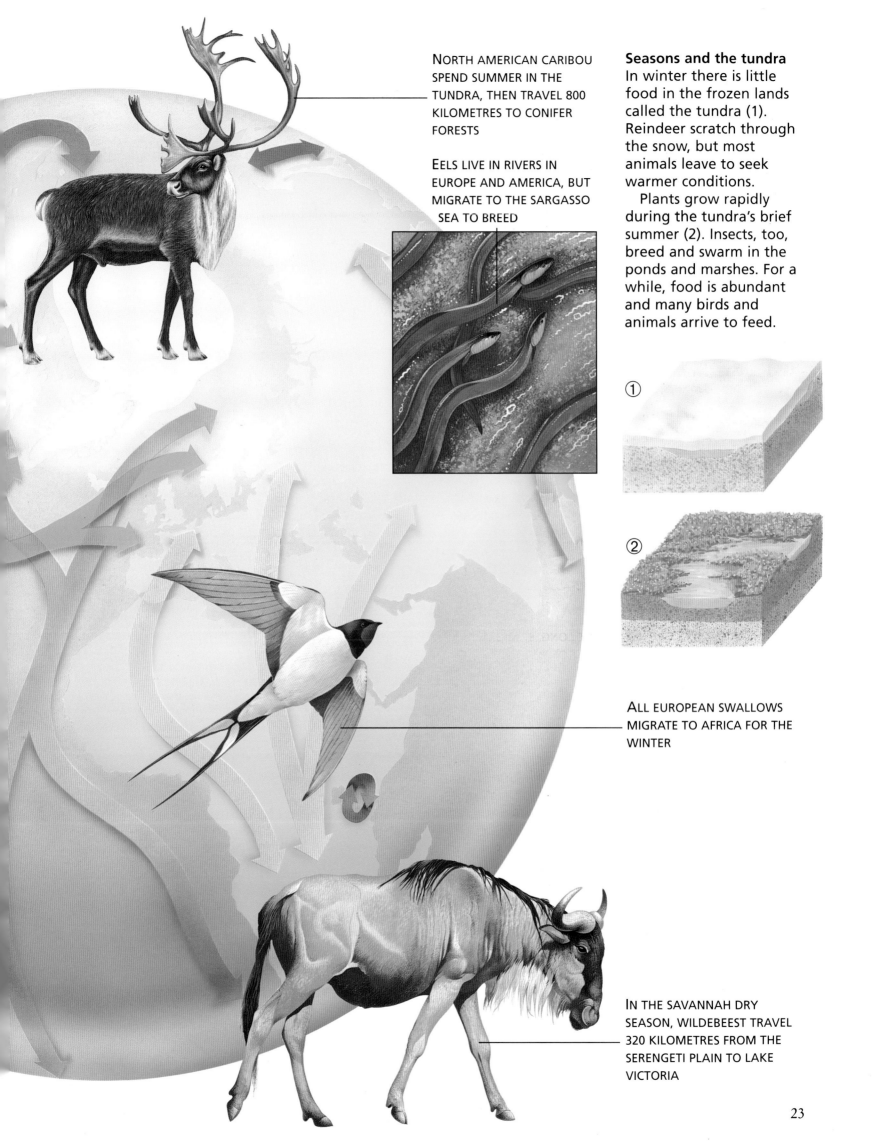

NORTH AMERICAN CARIBOU SPEND SUMMER IN THE TUNDRA, THEN TRAVEL 800 KILOMETRES TO CONIFER FORESTS

EELS LIVE IN RIVERS IN EUROPE AND AMERICA, BUT MIGRATE TO THE SARGASSO SEA TO BREED

Seasons and the tundra
In winter there is little food in the frozen lands called the tundra (1). Reindeer scratch through the snow, but most animals leave to seek warmer conditions.

Plants grow rapidly during the tundra's brief summer (2). Insects, too, breed and swarm in the ponds and marshes. For a while, food is abundant and many birds and animals arrive to feed.

①

②

ALL EUROPEAN SWALLOWS MIGRATE TO AFRICA FOR THE WINTER

IN THE SAVANNAH DRY SEASON, WILDEBEEST TRAVEL 320 KILOMETRES FROM THE SERENGETI PLAIN TO LAKE VICTORIA

23

Niches

ON A SINGLE OAK TREE THERE ARE HUNDREDS OF NICHES FOR OTHER PLANTS AND ANIMALS

THE CUCKOO IS A PARASITE – IT USES OTHER BIRDS TO RAISE ITS YOUNG; HERE IT IS THROWING OUT A BLACKBIRD'S EGG TO MAKE ROOM FOR ITS OWN IN THE NEST

THE WOODPECKER'S NEST

A WOODPECKER DRILLS INTO THE BARK TO FIND INSECTS

WHERE there is anything a living organism can eat or digest, and where there is shelter or enough space, sooner or later these resources will be put to use. The new arrival may be a plant, animal or colony of bacteria. Once settled in its home, the organism has created a 'niche', a place within the larger community of living things.

Find a stone that has been on the ground undisturbed for a long time and you may see lichen or moss growing on it. The plant has found a firm place to fix itself, obtaining the food it needs from the stone, and getting enough water from the moist air or rain. It has found its niche and, in doing so, the plant also provides niches for others, including the tiny animals that feed on it. On a single oak tree (*right*) there may be hundreds of niches.

A MOTH, WITH MARKINGS THAT MAKE IT ALMOST INVISIBLE, RESTS ON A PATCH OF LICHEN

LICHENS, FUNGI AND FERNS USE THE TREE'S BRANCHES AND TRUNK TO SUPPORT THEM

SQUIRRELS EAT ACORNS AND NEST HIGH ABOVE THE GROUND, WHERE THEY ARE SAFE

BANK VOLES FIND FOOD AND SHELTER IN THE GRASS AROUND TREE ROOTS

IN SPRING, CATERPILLARS FEED ON THE TREE'S LEAVES

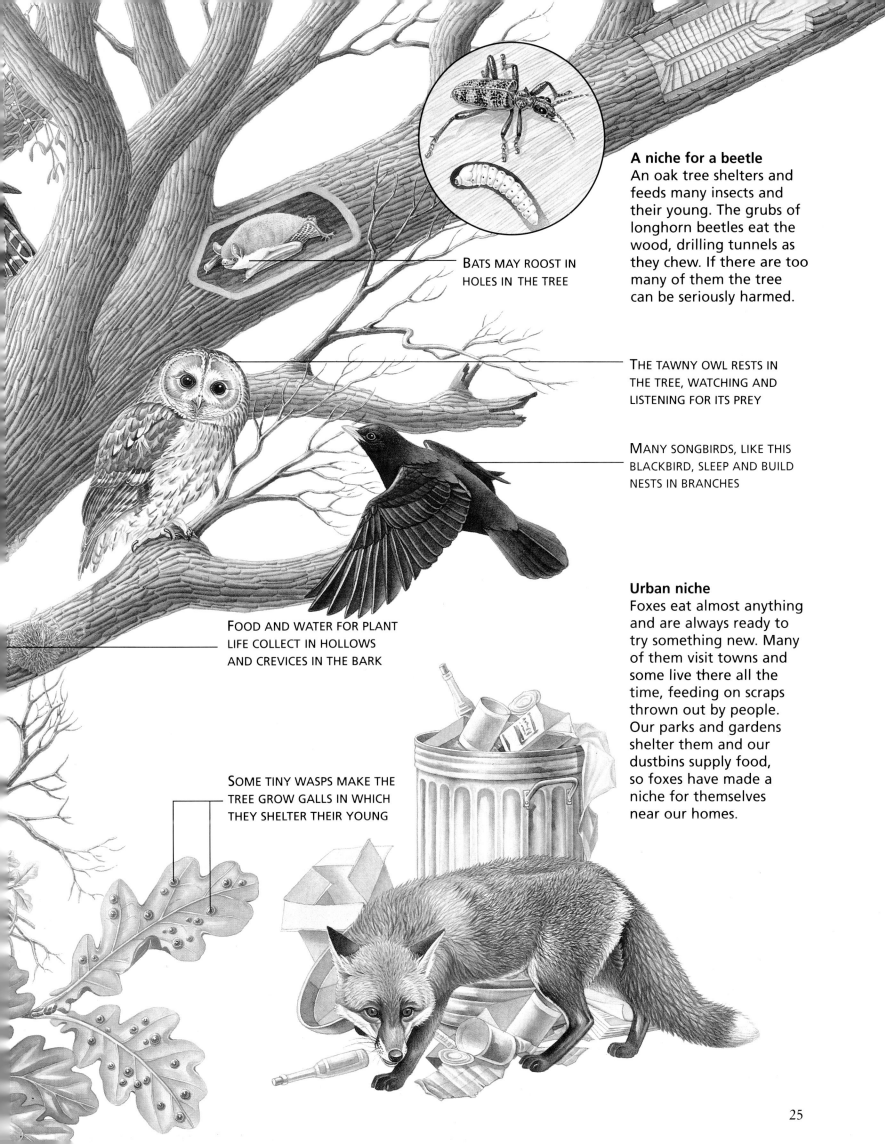

A niche for a beetle
An oak tree shelters and feeds many insects and their young. The grubs of longhorn beetles eat the wood, drilling tunnels as they chew. If there are too many of them the tree can be seriously harmed.

BATS MAY ROOST IN HOLES IN THE TREE

THE TAWNY OWL RESTS IN THE TREE, WATCHING AND LISTENING FOR ITS PREY

MANY SONGBIRDS, LIKE THIS BLACKBIRD, SLEEP AND BUILD NESTS IN BRANCHES

FOOD AND WATER FOR PLANT LIFE COLLECT IN HOLLOWS AND CREVICES IN THE BARK

Urban niche
Foxes eat almost anything and are always ready to try something new. Many of them visit towns and some live there all the time, feeding on scraps thrown out by people. Our parks and gardens shelter them and our dustbins supply food, so foxes have made a niche for themselves near our homes.

SOME TINY WASPS MAKE THE TREE GROW GALLS IN WHICH THEY SHELTER THEIR YOUNG

The Life Cycle of a Lake

AN AREA of land can go through many changes. For example, a lake can become dry land, and the dry land may eventually become woodland. At each stage a different group of plants and animals arrives to live there.

On these pages we can see how a community of living things has occupied a lake and its shores. We can also see the gradual build-up of mud and dead material on the lake bottom. These are signs that the lake will eventually become dry land. On the shoreline new plants are growing that take advantage of the build-up of mud. There are also insects and birds that find shelter in the new growth.

PLANTS GROW IN MUD, WASHED INTO THE LAKE BY RAIN OR CARRIED BY A RIVER

AS MUD COLLECTS, THE LAKE BECOMES SHALLOWER

SOME PLANTS FLOAT ON THE SURFACE, WITHOUT ROOTS

WATER LILIES ARE ROOTED IN THE LAKE BED – THEIR LEAVES FLOAT ON THE SURFACE

DEAD PLANTS SINK TO THE LAKE BOTTOM

LAKES FORM WHERE ROCK STOPS WATER FROM DRAINING DOWNWARDS

THE LAKE IS ALSO HOME TO FISH, LIKE THIS BREAM (*ABOVE*) AND PIKE (*RIGHT*)

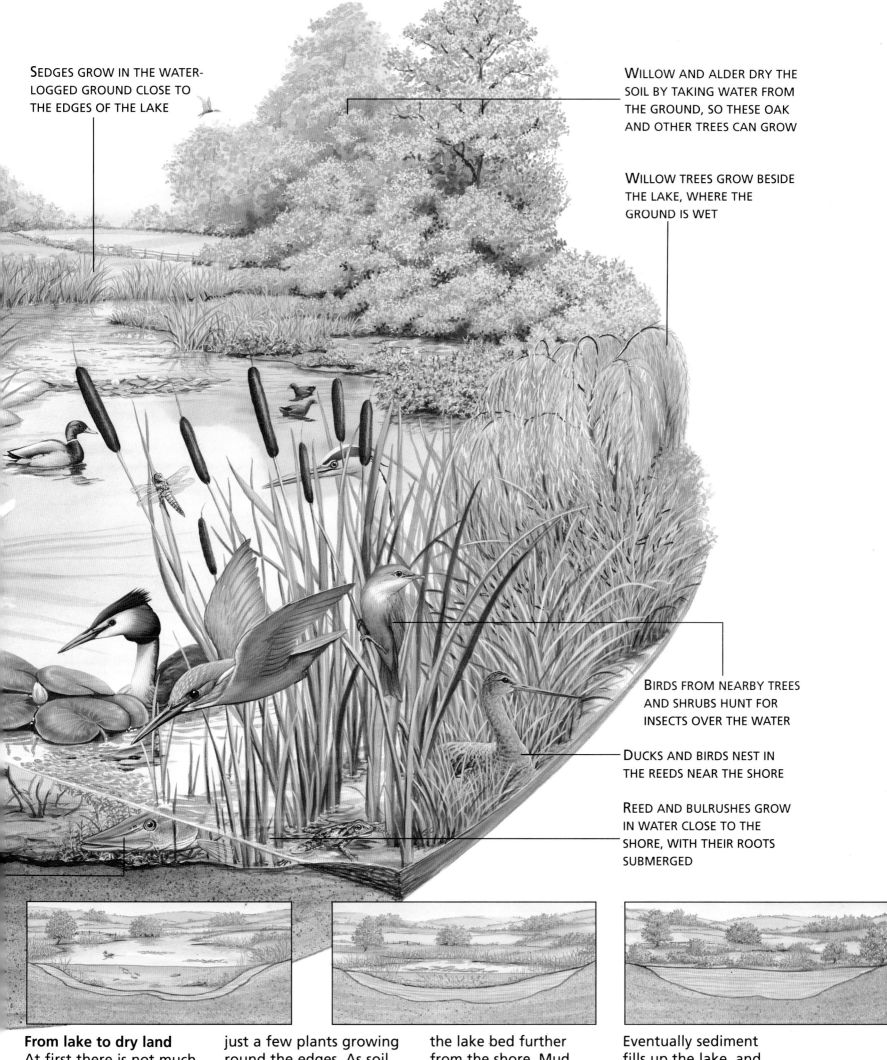

SEDGES GROW IN THE WATER-LOGGED GROUND CLOSE TO THE EDGES OF THE LAKE

WILLOW AND ALDER DRY THE SOIL BY TAKING WATER FROM THE GROUND, SO THESE OAK AND OTHER TREES CAN GROW

WILLOW TREES GROW BESIDE THE LAKE, WHERE THE GROUND IS WET

BIRDS FROM NEARBY TREES AND SHRUBS HUNT FOR INSECTS OVER THE WATER

DUCKS AND BIRDS NEST IN THE REEDS NEAR THE SHORE

REED AND BULRUSHES GROW IN WATER CLOSE TO THE SHORE, WITH THEIR ROOTS SUBMERGED

From lake to dry land
At first there is not much food for plants in the lake's water, so there are just a few plants growing round the edges. As soil washes in from nearby land, plants take root in the lake bed further from the shore. Mud and leaves build up, and more plants take root. Eventually sediment fills up the lake, and instead of a lake we see dry land.

Ecosystems

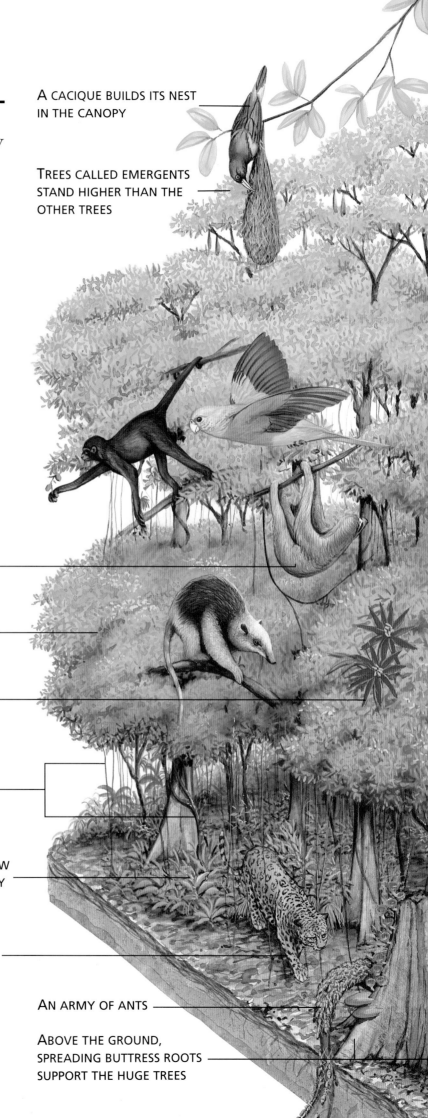

AN ECOSYSTEM is a community of plants and animals that live together, drawing on the same food and energy sources from their surroundings. If one community is different from others nearby, it can be studied by itself as an ecosystem.

Tropical rain forests are very rich ecosystems. They grow near the equator, where the climate is hot and wet. They can support many more kinds of plants and animals than are found in cooler climates. Plants grow rapidly and there is no cold or dry season to interrupt them. On this page we see how rain forests provide countless niches and many small ecosystems within the main forest ecosystem.

A CACIQUE BUILDS ITS NEST IN THE CANOPY

TREES CALLED EMERGENTS STAND HIGHER THAN THE OTHER TREES

THE TAMANDUA AND SLOTH LIVE IN THE CANOPY (TREE-TOPS), WHERE THERE IS MORE FOOD, SUCH AS FRUIT AND INSECTS

YOUNG TREES FORM A LOWER CANOPY

EPIPHYTES ARE PLANTS, OFTEN ROOTLESS, THAT GROW ON TREES – THIS IS A BROMELIAD

LIANAS ARE CLIMBERS THAT GROW UP TREES TOWARDS THE LIGHT – THEY HANG LIKE ROPES FROM THE BRANCHES

SAPLINGS AND SHRUBS GROW IN THE SHADY UNDERSTOREY

A JAGUAR HUNTS FOR ITS PREY ON THE DARK FOREST FLOOR

AN ARMY OF ANTS

ABOVE THE GROUND, SPREADING BUTTRESS ROOTS SUPPORT THE HUGE TREES

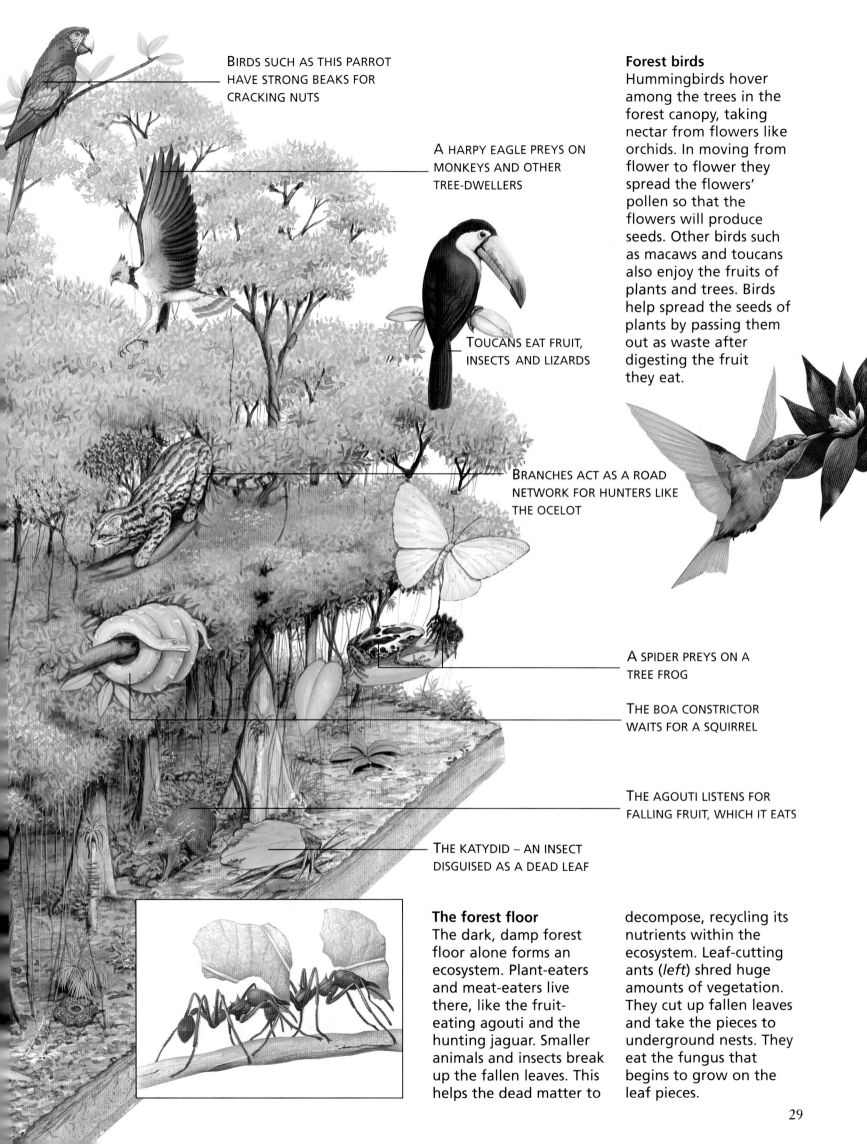

BIRDS SUCH AS THIS PARROT HAVE STRONG BEAKS FOR CRACKING NUTS

A HARPY EAGLE PREYS ON MONKEYS AND OTHER TREE-DWELLERS

TOUCANS EAT FRUIT, INSECTS AND LIZARDS

BRANCHES ACT AS A ROAD NETWORK FOR HUNTERS LIKE THE OCELOT

A SPIDER PREYS ON A TREE FROG

THE BOA CONSTRICTOR WAITS FOR A SQUIRREL

THE AGOUTI LISTENS FOR FALLING FRUIT, WHICH IT EATS

THE KATYDID – AN INSECT DISGUISED AS A DEAD LEAF

Forest birds

Hummingbirds hover among the trees in the forest canopy, taking nectar from flowers like orchids. In moving from flower to flower they spread the flowers' pollen so that the flowers will produce seeds. Other birds such as macaws and toucans also enjoy the fruits of plants and trees. Birds help spread the seeds of plants by passing them out as waste after digesting the fruit they eat.

The forest floor

The dark, damp forest floor alone forms an ecosystem. Plant-eaters and meat-eaters live there, like the fruit-eating agouti and the hunting jaguar. Smaller animals and insects break up the fallen leaves. This helps the dead matter to decompose, recycling its nutrients within the ecosystem. Leaf-cutting ants (*left*) shred huge amounts of vegetation. They cut up fallen leaves and take the pieces to underground nests. They eat the fungus that begins to grow on the leaf pieces.

Biomes

WHEN one type of ecosystem covers a vast area it is called a biome. Different climates produce different biomes. There are several biomes in Africa, including tropical rain forest, savannah grassland and desert. A desert biome, such as the Sahara in Africa, forms where there is little rain. Here, temperatures run to extremes, so it can be freezing at night after being extremely hot during the day. Bordering the Sahara desert are savannah grasslands which are also warm and dry, but, unlike the deserts, heavy rains fall here in late spring.

Biomes map
mixed forest
mountain
grassland
tropical rain forest
semi-desert
desert

IN THE SAHARA DAY-TIME TEMPERATURES ARE AROUND 40°C

LESS THAN 50 MM OF RAIN A YEAR FALLS IN PARTS OF THE SAHARA

SAND STORMS OCCUR WHEN STRONG WINDS LIFT DUST AND SAND HIGH INTO THE AIR

FENNEC FOX

JERBOA

THE SAHARA HAS VAST SAND SEAS CALLED ERGS BUT IN PARTS THE LAND IS ROCKY

PLANTS WITH LONG ROOTS FIND WATER DEEP UNDERGROUND

CAMELS CAN SURVIVE WITHOUT WATER FOR MORE THAN TWO WEEKS

DESERT SOIL IS THIN

Desert animals
Animals have adapted to the desert climate. Lizards and jerboa shelter from the heat in burrows. The fennec fox and jerboa (*see above*) have large ears rich in blood veins, which helps them lose body heat. Ostriches can drink the desert's salty water and do not suffer if their body temperature rises.

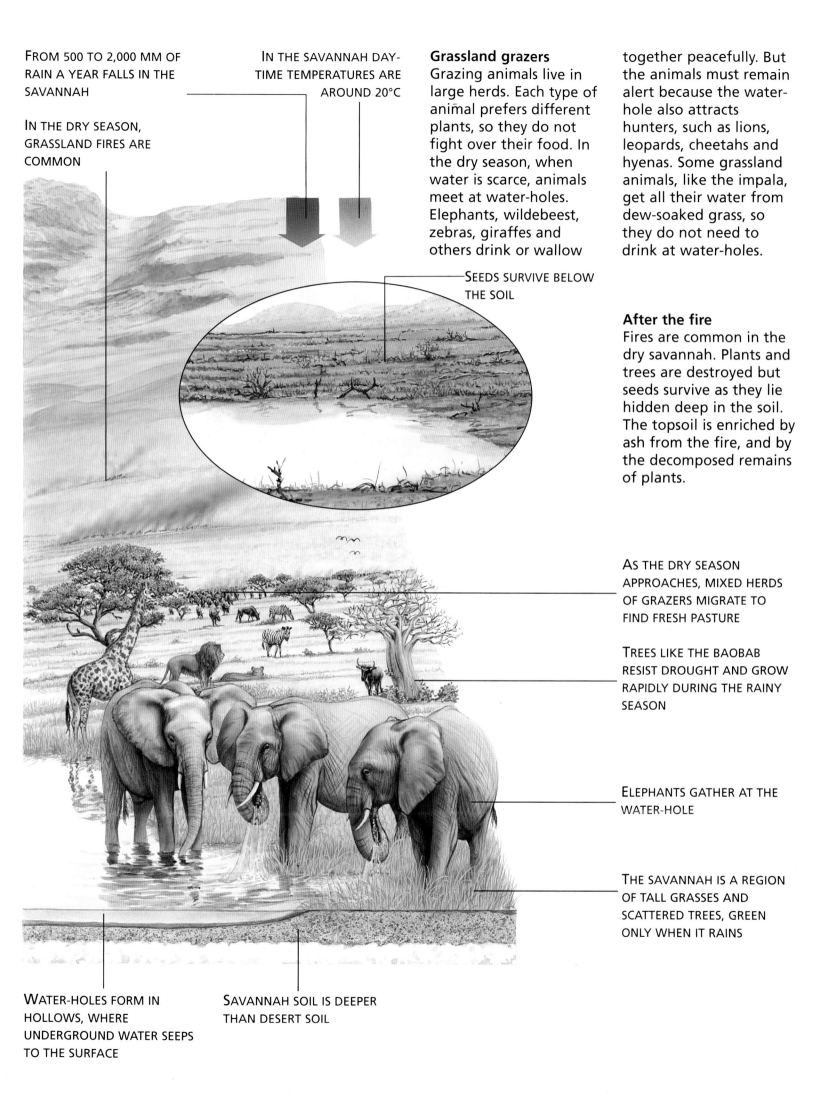

FROM 500 TO 2,000 MM OF RAIN A YEAR FALLS IN THE SAVANNAH

IN THE DRY SEASON, GRASSLAND FIRES ARE COMMON

IN THE SAVANNAH DAY-TIME TEMPERATURES ARE AROUND 20°C

Grassland grazers

Grazing animals live in large herds. Each type of animal prefers different plants, so they do not fight over their food. In the dry season, when water is scarce, animals meet at water-holes. Elephants, wildebeest, zebras, giraffes and others drink or wallow together peacefully. But the animals must remain alert because the water-hole also attracts hunters, such as lions, leopards, cheetahs and hyenas. Some grassland animals, like the impala, get all their water from dew-soaked grass, so they do not need to drink at water-holes.

SEEDS SURVIVE BELOW THE SOIL

After the fire

Fires are common in the dry savannah. Plants and trees are destroyed but seeds survive as they lie hidden deep in the soil. The topsoil is enriched by ash from the fire, and by the decomposed remains of plants.

AS THE DRY SEASON APPROACHES, MIXED HERDS OF GRAZERS MIGRATE TO FIND FRESH PASTURE

TREES LIKE THE BAOBAB RESIST DROUGHT AND GROW RAPIDLY DURING THE RAINY SEASON

ELEPHANTS GATHER AT THE WATER-HOLE

THE SAVANNAH IS A REGION OF TALL GRASSES AND SCATTERED TREES, GREEN ONLY WHEN IT RAINS

WATER-HOLES FORM IN HOLLOWS, WHERE UNDERGROUND WATER SEEPS TO THE SURFACE

SAVANNAH SOIL IS DEEPER THAN DESERT SOIL

Nutrient Cycles

ALL living things, including people, are made of about 20 chemical elements, such as carbon, nitrogen, calcium and sulphur. Plants and animals use these 'nutrients' to build their cells and to provide energy, and must regularly top them up. The nutrients come from the environment – from rocks and from the air. Plants absorb water and mineral nutrients such as sulphur and calcium from the soil. They absorb carbon from the air. Animals take in their nutrients by eating plants or other animals.

All nutrients follow cycles and are returned to the environment, so new living things can live and grow. If nutrients did not move through cycles, soon there would be none left and all life would cease.

The sulphur cycle
The large illustration shows how the nutrient sulphur follows a cycle. Sulphur is taken up from rocks by plants, and passes to animals that eat the plants. Animal wastes and dead animal and plant matter decompose and sulphur is returned to the ground. It is then carried away by groundwater and rivers to the sea. Some sulphur is trapped in mud in estuaries. Here, bacteria release the sulphur in a different form back into the air. Most of the sulphur is taken in by tiny sea plants called plankton. These also release the sulphur in a different form back into the air. Sulphur in the air eventually falls back to the ground in rain.

Volcanoes release extra sulphur from beneath the Earth's crust into the air. They return some of the sulphur that is trapped deep underground to the sulphur cycle.

BACTERIA LIVING IN MUDS AND MARSHES RELEASE A COMPOUND OF SULPHUR (HYDROGEN SULPHIDE)

SULPHUR (IN VARIOUS CHEMICAL FORMS OR COMPOUNDS) DISSOLVES INTO RAIN DROPS

SULPHUR IS RETURNED TO THE LAND IN RAIN

NUTRIENTS IN DEAD PLANTS AND ANIMALS ARE RELEASED BACK INTO THE GROUND THROUGH DECOMPOSITION

SULPHUR IS TAKEN UP BY LIVING PLANTS AND ANIMALS

SULPHUR ORIGINALLY COMES FROM ROCK

ANIMALS AND HUMAN BEINGS NEED SULPHUR TO MAKE PROTEINS (SKIN AND HAIR CONTAIN SULPHUR)

GROUNDWATER AND RIVERS TAKE SULPHUR TO THE SEA

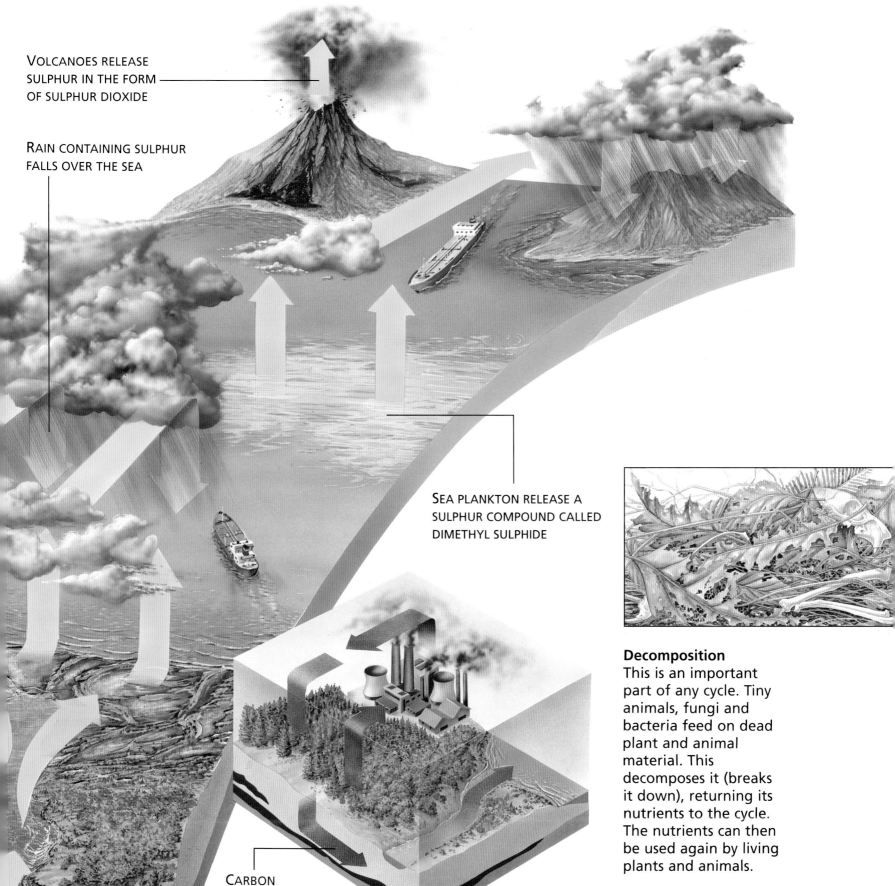

VOLCANOES RELEASE SULPHUR IN THE FORM OF SULPHUR DIOXIDE

RAIN CONTAINING SULPHUR FALLS OVER THE SEA

SEA PLANKTON RELEASE A SULPHUR COMPOUND CALLED DIMETHYL SULPHIDE

CARBON

Decomposition
This is an important part of any cycle. Tiny animals, fungi and bacteria feed on dead plant and animal material. This decomposes it (breaks it down), returning its nutrients to the cycle. The nutrients can then be used again by living plants and animals.

The carbon cycle
Green plants absorb carbon dioxide from the air during photosynthesis. Living things other than plants take in carbon by eating plants or by eating other animals. During the decomposition of dead plant and animal material, carbon is released back into the air as carbon dioxide. Carbon dioxide also enters the air during respiration (when animals breathe out, they release carbon dioxide; plants release it too). Carbon dioxide also escapes into the air when we burn carbon fuels such as coal, gas and oil. Tiny marine plants and shellfish also play a major part in the carbon cycle (*see pages 14–15*).

Obtaining Nitrogen

THE AIR IS MOSTLY NITROGEN GAS

A NUTRIENT cycle involves many complicated chemical changes. This is especially true of the nitrogen cycle. Although there is plenty of nitrogen in the air, there is a problem. Plants and animals cannot use nitrogen as a gas; they must have it in the form of food. This means the gas has to be changed into nitrogen compounds, such as nitrates. Bacteria in the soil do this complicated job. They change nitrogen into nitrates, which plants can then use to make proteins (the chemical 'building blocks' from which plant and animal bodies are made). Late in the cycle, animals take in the nitrates when they eat the plants.

ENERGY FROM LIGHTNING CHANGES NITROGEN GAS INTO A COMPOUND THAT DISSOLVES IN WATER

NITROGEN COMPOUNDS FALL TO THE SOIL IN RAIN WATER

NITRATES IN WATER ENTER PLANT ROOTS AND FEED THE PLANT

The nitrogen cycle
Nitrates in the soil-water are drawn up through the roots of plants. The plants use the nitrates to make proteins. Animals that eat the plants change the plant proteins into animal proteins.

Animal and plant wastes contain proteins and other nitrogen compounds. So when they decompose, the nitrogen compounds are once more available to plants. Some bacteria, called 'denitrifying' bacteria (*right*), break down nitrogen compounds and release nitrogen gas back into the air.

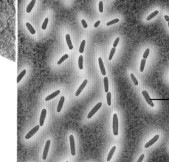

DENITRIFYING BACTERIA

34

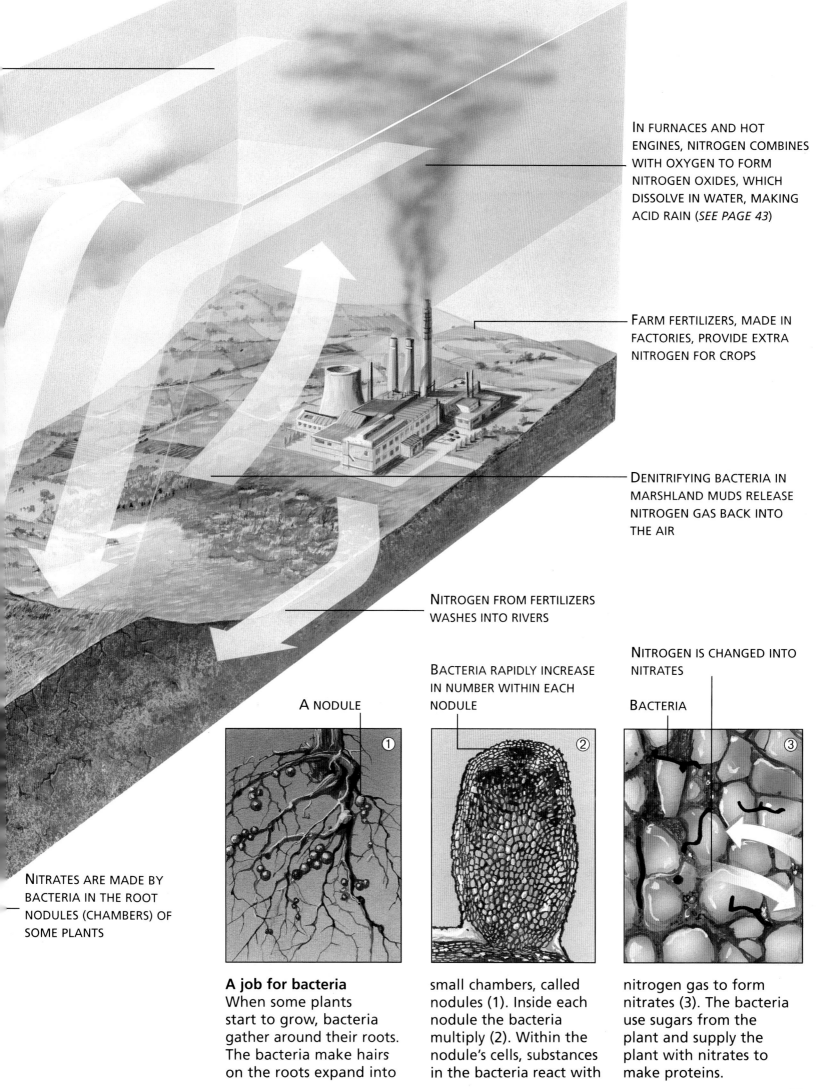

IN FURNACES AND HOT ENGINES, NITROGEN COMBINES WITH OXYGEN TO FORM NITROGEN OXIDES, WHICH DISSOLVE IN WATER, MAKING ACID RAIN (*SEE PAGE 43*)

FARM FERTILIZERS, MADE IN FACTORIES, PROVIDE EXTRA NITROGEN FOR CROPS

DENITRIFYING BACTERIA IN MARSHLAND MUDS RELEASE NITROGEN GAS BACK INTO THE AIR

NITROGEN FROM FERTILIZERS WASHES INTO RIVERS

NITRATES ARE MADE BY BACTERIA IN THE ROOT NODULES (CHAMBERS) OF SOME PLANTS

A NODULE

BACTERIA RAPIDLY INCREASE IN NUMBER WITHIN EACH NODULE

NITROGEN IS CHANGED INTO NITRATES

BACTERIA

A job for bacteria
When some plants start to grow, bacteria gather around their roots. The bacteria make hairs on the roots expand into small chambers, called nodules (1). Inside each nodule the bacteria multiply (2). Within the nodule's cells, substances in the bacteria react with nitrogen gas to form nitrates (3). The bacteria use sugars from the plant and supply the plant with nitrates to make proteins.

Soil

SOIL is made up of tiny pieces of rock and the decayed remains of dead organisms. The rock fragments have appeared after thousands of years of weathering. Near the surface of the land, the heat of summer makes rocks expand and the cold of winter makes them shrink. This causes the rocks to crack, and rainwater then trickles into the cracks. In winter the water freezes and expands, widening the cracks and causing fragments of rock to break off. Acids in the water weaken the rock so that it breaks apart more easily. Rocks deeper underground are weakened by water that seeps up from below. All these processes, called weathering, help to make soil by breaking up the rock.

MOST SOILS FORM AS DISTINCT LAYERS, LYING ONE ABOVE THE OTHER

WATER MOVES BETWEEN THE PARTICLES OF SOIL

Water in soil
Rainwater moves down from the earth's surface between rock particles until it can go no further. This water under the ground is called groundwater and its upper surface is called the water table. As water dries on the surface of the soil (evaporating into the air) it is replaced by groundwater, drawn upwards through very small spaces. This upward movement of water keeps the soil moist.

MANY TREES HAVE ROOT SYSTEMS AS LARGE AS THE TRUNK AND BRANCHES SEEN ABOVE GROUND

PLANTS GROW WELL IN SOILS THAT CONTAIN PLENTY OF NUTRIENTS (FERTILE SOILS)

ACCORDING TO THE TYPE OF ROCK, SOILS CAN BE SANDY OR CLAYEY

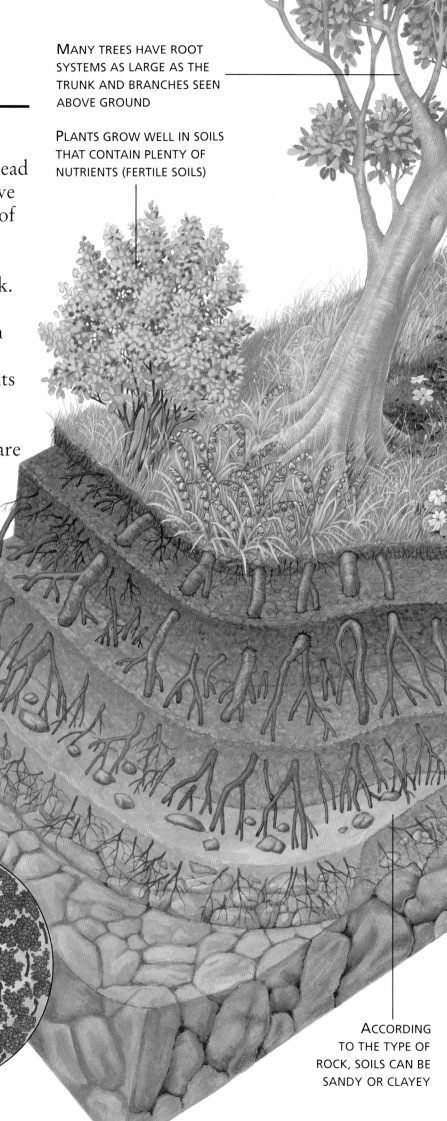

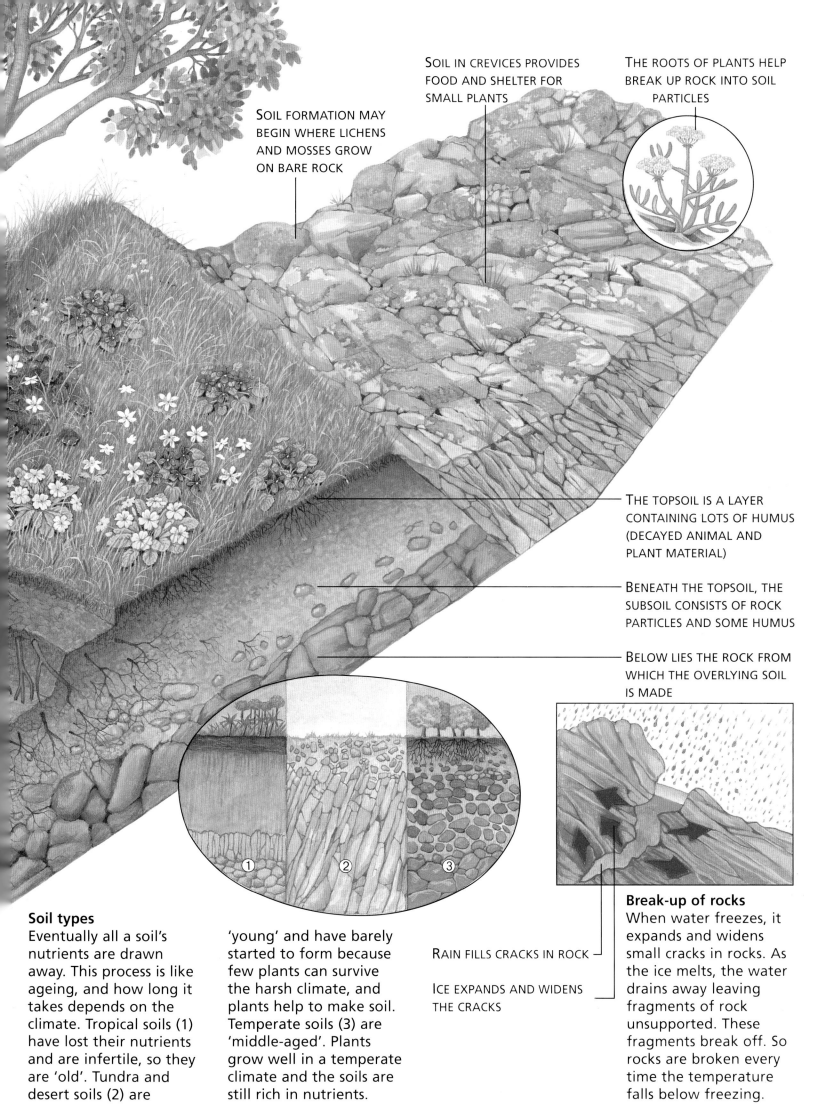

SOIL FORMATION MAY BEGIN WHERE LICHENS AND MOSSES GROW ON BARE ROCK

SOIL IN CREVICES PROVIDES FOOD AND SHELTER FOR SMALL PLANTS

THE ROOTS OF PLANTS HELP BREAK UP ROCK INTO SOIL PARTICLES

THE TOPSOIL IS A LAYER CONTAINING LOTS OF HUMUS (DECAYED ANIMAL AND PLANT MATERIAL)

BENEATH THE TOPSOIL, THE SUBSOIL CONSISTS OF ROCK PARTICLES AND SOME HUMUS

BELOW LIES THE ROCK FROM WHICH THE OVERLYING SOIL IS MADE

RAIN FILLS CRACKS IN ROCK

ICE EXPANDS AND WIDENS THE CRACKS

Soil types

Eventually all a soil's nutrients are drawn away. This process is like ageing, and how long it takes depends on the climate. Tropical soils (1) have lost their nutrients and are infertile, so they are 'old'. Tundra and desert soils (2) are 'young' and have barely started to form because few plants can survive the harsh climate, and plants help to make soil. Temperate soils (3) are 'middle-aged'. Plants grow well in a temperate climate and the soils are still rich in nutrients.

Break-up of rocks

When water freezes, it expands and widens small cracks in rocks. As the ice melts, the water drains away leaving fragments of rock unsupported. These fragments break off. So rocks are broken every time the temperature falls below freezing.

Soil Life

THE organisms living in the top few centimetres of soil in a field of grass may weigh more than the cows grazing the pasture. A fertile soil teems with life, from single-celled bacteria to animals the size of moles. Each organism occupies its own niche within the soil ecosystem. Woodlice, for example, eat decaying plant matter and their droppings provide tiny bits of simpler food for smaller organisms.

By living in or on the surface of the soil, organisms actually help to make more soil. They do this by eating and breaking down animal and plant materials.

Mites
There are more mites than any other type of soil animal. Mites are tiny relatives of spiders. Plant-eating mites break leaves into smaller pieces (*see below*). Other mites hunt animals such as nematodes.

FUNGI BREAK DOWN WOOD

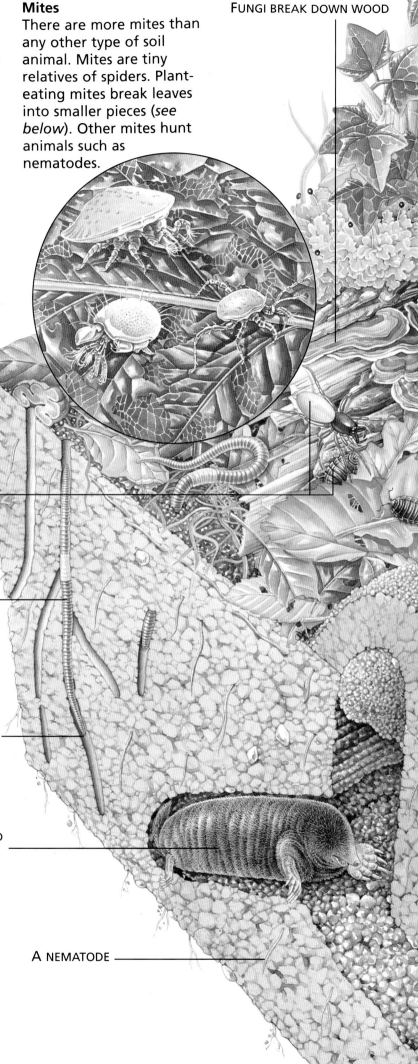

A SPIDER HUNTS FOR LICE

EARTHWORMS SURFACE AT NIGHT TO DEPOSIT THEIR CASTS (WASTE MATTER)

WORM TUNNELS GIVE ROOM FOR AIR TO CIRCULATE IN THE SOIL

THE MOLE DIGS LONG TUNNELS, EATING WORMS AND OTHER ANIMALS THAT FALL INTO THEM

A NEMATODE

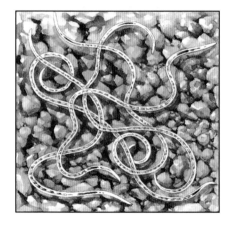

Nematodes
There are a vast number of nematodes (eelworms) in the soil. There may be a million of them living in the first 10 centimetres below a square metre of the surface. They are thread-like and the largest are barely 2 millimetres long (*see above*). They live in the soil water and eat other nematodes or single-celled organisms such as bacteria. Nematodes help control the size of the microscopic soil population.

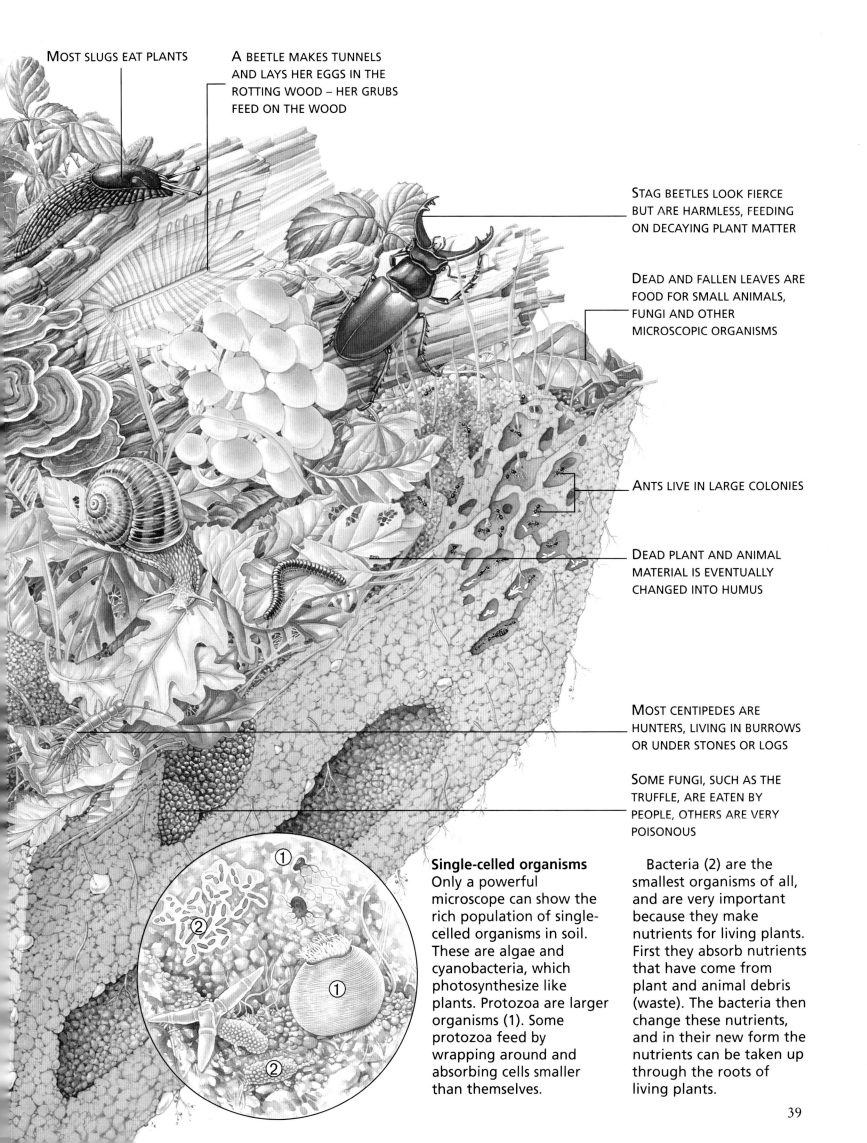

MOST SLUGS EAT PLANTS

A BEETLE MAKES TUNNELS AND LAYS HER EGGS IN THE ROTTING WOOD – HER GRUBS FEED ON THE WOOD

STAG BEETLES LOOK FIERCE BUT ARE HARMLESS, FEEDING ON DECAYING PLANT MATTER

DEAD AND FALLEN LEAVES ARE FOOD FOR SMALL ANIMALS, FUNGI AND OTHER MICROSCOPIC ORGANISMS

ANTS LIVE IN LARGE COLONIES

DEAD PLANT AND ANIMAL MATERIAL IS EVENTUALLY CHANGED INTO HUMUS

MOST CENTIPEDES ARE HUNTERS, LIVING IN BURROWS OR UNDER STONES OR LOGS

SOME FUNGI, SUCH AS THE TRUFFLE, ARE EATEN BY PEOPLE, OTHERS ARE VERY POISONOUS

Single-celled organisms
Only a powerful microscope can show the rich population of single-celled organisms in soil. These are algae and cyanobacteria, which photosynthesize like plants. Protozoa are larger organisms (1). Some protozoa feed by wrapping around and absorbing cells smaller than themselves.

Bacteria (2) are the smallest organisms of all, and are very important because they make nutrients for living plants. First they absorb nutrients that have come from plant and animal debris (waste). The bacteria then change these nutrients, and in their new form the nutrients can be taken up through the roots of living plants.

39

Rivers

WHEN rainwater falls on bare rock or thin soil, it flows downhill across the surface of the land. If the soil is deep, the rainwater first soaks downwards until it meets rock before it flows downhill. This underground water is called groundwater. In hollows, where rocks are closer to the surface, it runs out as a spring.

On the surface of the land, water flows along channels. A small channel of water is called a stream. The water wears away at the channel, making it deeper. As more water joins the channel from high ground or springs, the tiny stream grows into a river. The river is home to many plants and animals which live in distinct zones: the headwaters, the troutbeck, the minnow reach, the bream zone, and the estuary.

Minnow zone
The river slows as it leaves the hills. Sediment (mud) collects on the stony bottom, and plants take root in it. This is the minnow, or grayling zone. Minnows and graylings feed on small animals such as young fish and insects.

PLANTS SUCH AS THESE TAKE ROOT IN THE RIVER SEDIMENT

ON ALMOST LEVEL GROUND, THE RIVER MEANDERS (ITS PATH TWISTS FROM SIDE TO SIDE)

Estuary zone
An estuary is where a river widens and meets the sea. The incoming tide brings salty sea water upstream. Where the sea and river waters mix, tiny particles sink to form mudbanks. The sea may deposit sand. Worms and other small animals feed in the mud. They in turn are food for wading birds. The heron hunts for fish in the shallow water (*see below*).

THE LAND IS NEARLY FLAT HERE – IT IS CALLED THE FLOOD PLAIN

THE RIVER FLOWS OUT TO SEA

SEDIMENT BUILDS UP INTO A MUDBANK

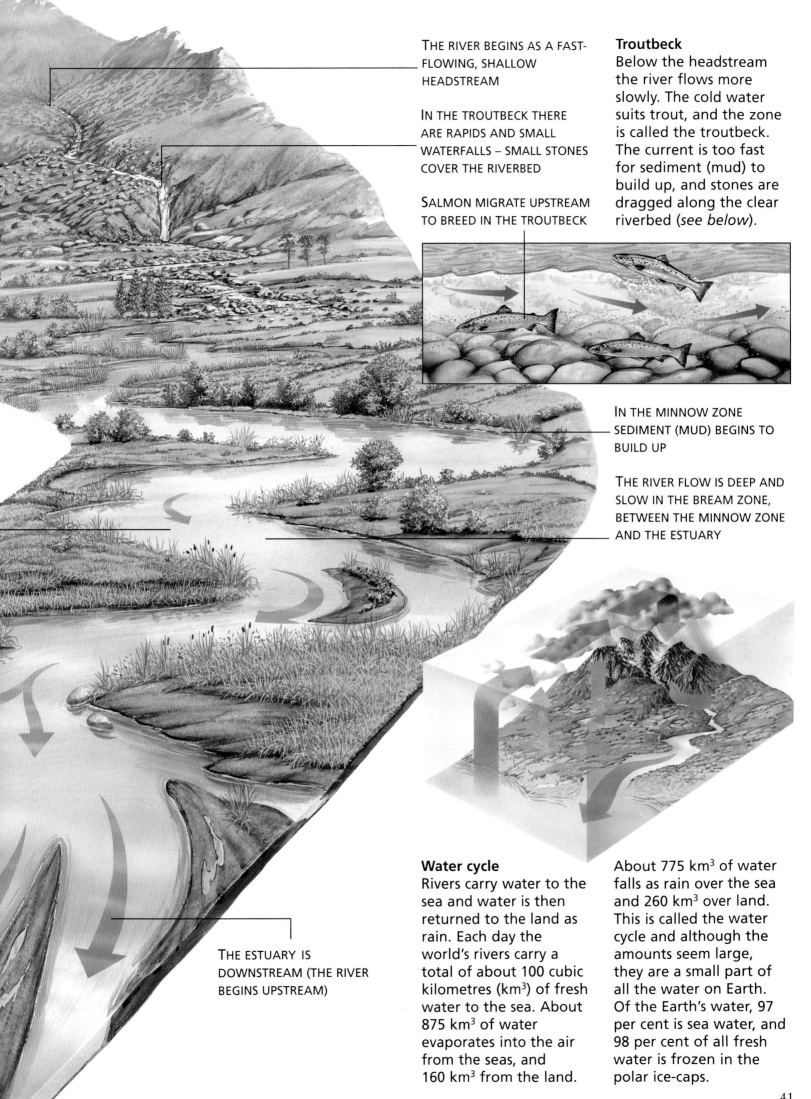

THE RIVER BEGINS AS A FAST-FLOWING, SHALLOW HEADSTREAM

IN THE TROUTBECK THERE ARE RAPIDS AND SMALL WATERFALLS – SMALL STONES COVER THE RIVERBED

SALMON MIGRATE UPSTREAM TO BREED IN THE TROUTBECK

Troutbeck
Below the headstream the river flows more slowly. The cold water suits trout, and the zone is called the troutbeck. The current is too fast for sediment (mud) to build up, and stones are dragged along the clear riverbed (*see below*).

IN THE MINNOW ZONE SEDIMENT (MUD) BEGINS TO BUILD UP

THE RIVER FLOW IS DEEP AND SLOW IN THE BREAM ZONE, BETWEEN THE MINNOW ZONE AND THE ESTUARY

THE ESTUARY IS DOWNSTREAM (THE RIVER BEGINS UPSTREAM)

Water cycle
Rivers carry water to the sea and water is then returned to the land as rain. Each day the world's rivers carry a total of about 100 cubic kilometres (km³) of fresh water to the sea. About 875 km³ of water evaporates into the air from the seas, and 160 km³ from the land.

About 775 km³ of water falls as rain over the sea and 260 km³ over land. This is called the water cycle and although the amounts seem large, they are a small part of all the water on Earth. Of the Earth's water, 97 per cent is sea water, and 98 per cent of all fresh water is frozen in the polar ice-caps.

41

Environmental Damage

WE CANNOT avoid altering our environment and many of the changes we make are beneficial. But a lot of human activities do harm the environment. Clearing rain forests or other natural vegetation to make farmland reduces animal and plant habitats. The plants and animals become confined to smaller and smaller areas, and some species can die out all together. Waste products from our homes and factories can pollute the air, oceans and rivers. Pollution can poison organisms directly, or indirectly by damaging their environment.

Nowhere to live
Golden lion tamarins are tree-dwellers in the tropical forests of South America. When the trees are felled there is nowhere for them to live. There are fewer than 300 left in the wild. Soon the species may die out.

ABOUT 41,000 SQUARE KILOMETRES OF TROPICAL RAIN FOREST ARE CLEARED EACH YEAR (AN AREA BIGGER THAN SWITZERLAND)

TRADITIONAL FARMERS FELL TREES AND BURN THE VEGETATION THEY CANNOT USE

FOREST IS CLEARED TO ALLOW MINING FOR MINERALS

ONCE ROADS ARE BUILT, POOR FARMERS MOVE INTO THE FOREST AND CLEAR THE LAND TO GROW CROPS

THE SOIL IS POOR AND CROPS OFTEN FAIL

IN SOME PLACES CLEARED GROUND BECOMES AS HARD AS CONCRETE

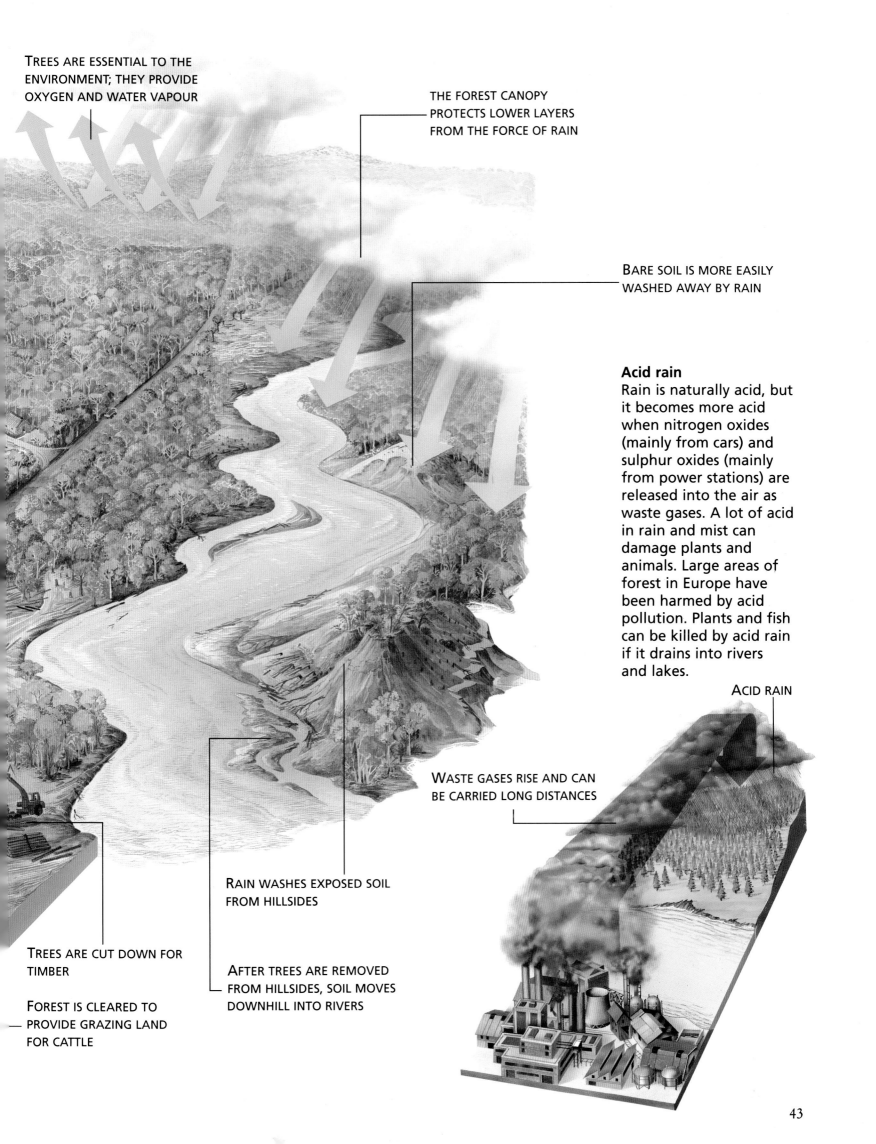

TREES ARE ESSENTIAL TO THE ENVIRONMENT; THEY PROVIDE OXYGEN AND WATER VAPOUR

THE FOREST CANOPY PROTECTS LOWER LAYERS FROM THE FORCE OF RAIN

BARE SOIL IS MORE EASILY WASHED AWAY BY RAIN

Acid rain
Rain is naturally acid, but it becomes more acid when nitrogen oxides (mainly from cars) and sulphur oxides (mainly from power stations) are released into the air as waste gases. A lot of acid in rain and mist can damage plants and animals. Large areas of forest in Europe have been harmed by acid pollution. Plants and fish can be killed by acid rain if it drains into rivers and lakes.

ACID RAIN

WASTE GASES RISE AND CAN BE CARRIED LONG DISTANCES

RAIN WASHES EXPOSED SOIL FROM HILLSIDES

TREES ARE CUT DOWN FOR TIMBER

AFTER TREES ARE REMOVED FROM HILLSIDES, SOIL MOVES DOWNHILL INTO RIVERS

FOREST IS CLEARED TO PROVIDE GRAZING LAND FOR CATTLE

43

Learning to Live in Harmony

TODAY most large industrial companies take care to cause as little environmental damage as possible. Many are working to restore areas that were damaged in the past.

Mines, such as the china clay mine seen below, can destroy wildlife and produce large waste tips. For every tonne of china clay taken out of the land, there are nine tonnes of waste. But even the large waste tips from a china clay mine can be transformed into green hills. Once the mining has finished, the whole area can be made into a local amenity, such as playing fields or a golf course. The hills may become grazing land for sheep. The illustrations on these pages show how this is done.

GRASS AND OTHER PLANT SEEDS ARE MIXED IN WATER AND SPRAYED ONTO THE TERRACES

ON THE SLOPES THE WASTE IS SHAPED INTO LONG FLAT TERRACES

RESTORATION WORK BEGINS AS SOON AS THE MINING IS FINISHED

AS THE CLAY IS MINED, WASTE IS PILED UP TO FORM UGLY PYRAMIDS

CHINA CLAY HAS MANY USES – THE PAPER IN THIS BOOK CONTAINS IT

TO GET AT THE CLAY A HUGE PIT HAS TO BE DUG

THE CLAY IS WASHED FROM THE ROCK BY HIGH-PRESSURE WATER HOSES

Polluted rivers
In the past, waste from the mine escaped into nearby rivers, colouring them white (1). With modern management the wastes are now held back and the rivers are their natural colour again (2).

THE PYRAMIDS OF WASTE ARE
FLATTENED ON TOP

LARGE MACHINES RESHAPE
THE LANDSCAPE

Putting vegetation back
Nitrate-producing plants,
such as clover (*below*),
are included in seed
mixtures to put nitrogen
back into the soil. Alder
trees can be planted to
help remove surplus
water. While the mining
is going on, wastes can
be used to build large
banks. Trees can be
grown on the banks to
hide the mine and shield
villagers from the dust.

Alaska pipeline
In Alaska, a pipeline was
needed to carry oil and
gas from the north to
the south. Because
it crossed the caribou
migration route (*see
pages 22–23*), it was built
on stilts so caribou could
pass underneath. Raising
the pipe also stopped it
from melting the frozen
soil. Damage to the
frozen soil would affect
the area's wildlife.

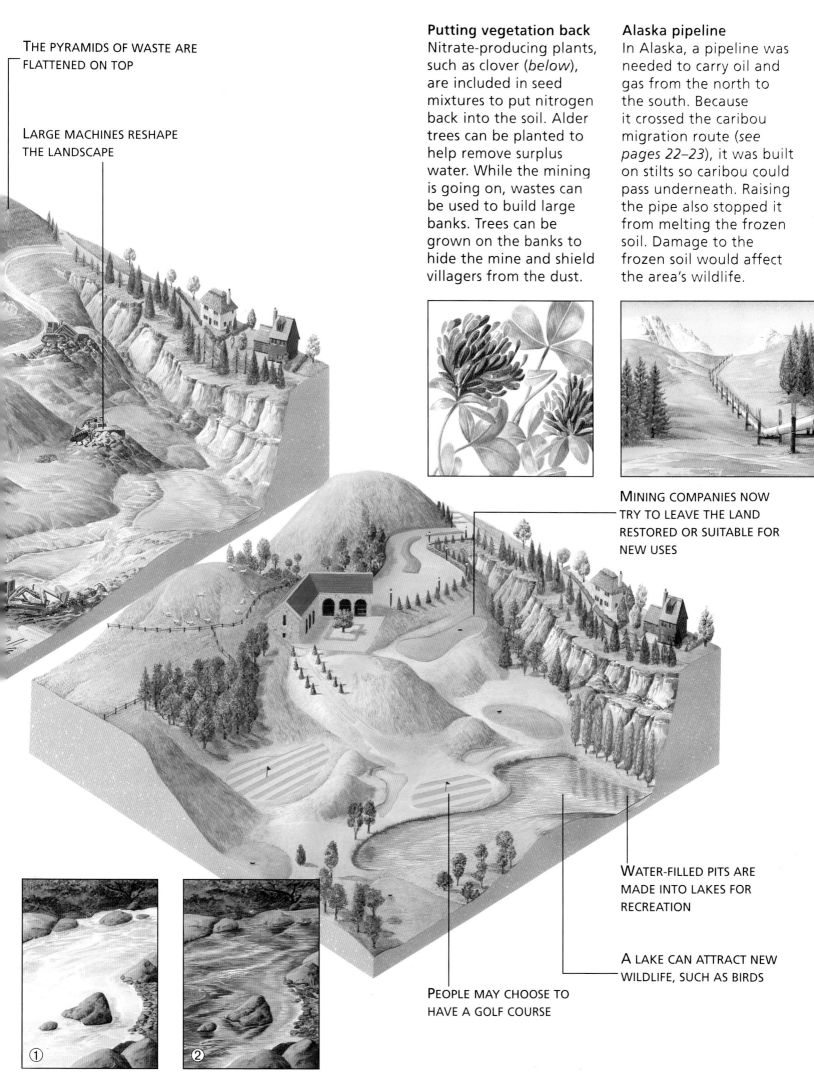

MINING COMPANIES NOW
TRY TO LEAVE THE LAND
RESTORED OR SUITABLE FOR
NEW USES

WATER-FILLED PITS ARE
MADE INTO LAKES FOR
RECREATION

A LAKE CAN ATTRACT NEW
WILDLIFE, SUCH AS BIRDS

PEOPLE MAY CHOOSE TO
HAVE A GOLF COURSE

① ②

Index